With compliments of

GEORGE WATSON COLE.

Graham Court, 1925 Seventh Ave.,
New York City.

Kindly acknowledge receipt.

LIBRARIES

OF

GREATER NEW YORK

MANUAL AND HISTORICAL SKETCH

OF THE

NEW YORK LIBRARY CLUB

NEW YORK

1902

PREFACE.

The List of libraries was in type in October, 1901, when the receipt of advance sheets from the Report of the United States Commissioner of Education for 1899–1900, giving statistics of "Public, society and school libraries," and of the "Annual report, 1900," on Public libraries, issued by the University of the State of New York, brought to light a number of libraries in New York City of which the Committee had no previous knowledge, although every available source of information had been examined. Some two hundred additional circulars of inquiry were sent out, and as a result more than one hundred libraries were added. In several instances repeated calls for information were not responded to; these libraries are indicated in the List by an asterisk (*) preceding the name.

The Committee is indebted to its chairman for compiling the List of libraries, to Mr. Nelson for the "Historical sketch" and the other historical matter in the "Manual," and to Mr. Bostwick for the List of "Members" of the Club.

Thanks are due and are cordially tendered to all who have aided the Committee in the compilation of this record of library progress in New York City.

George Watson Cole,
Charles Alexander Nelson,
Arthur Elmore Bostwick.

March 3, 1902.

Libraries of the City of New York

Academy of Medicine, New York. *See* New York Academy of Medicine.

* **Academy of Mount St. Vincent Library,** Kingsbridge, New York City. Miss Margaret M. Maher, Librarian. 1

HISTORY.—Founded 1846; school library; supported by the Academy; income for 1900, $128.

REGULATIONS.—Open 300 days in the year; 12 hours each week for circulation and 50 hours for reference; privileges restricted.

RESOURCES.—7165 vols.

Academy of Sciences, New York. *See* New York Academy of Sciences.

Adelphi College Library, Clifton Place, cor. St. James Place, Brooklyn, N. Y. Miss Mabel Farr, Librarian. 2

HISTORY.—Founded 1869; supported from public money and gifts; income for 1900, $325. Historical notice in "History of Brooklyn," published by the "Brooklyn Daily Eagle."

REGULATIONS.—Open session days, 8.30 A.M.–4 P.M.; reference and circulating; privileges extended only to pupils and teachers of Adelphi College and Adelphi Academy.

RESOURCES.—8530 vols.; a general collection.

**NOTE.*—An asterisk indicates that the information given was procured elsewhere than directly from the Library named.

Aguilar Free Library, 197 East Broadway, New York City. Miss Pauline Leipziger, Librarian; Dr. Henry Marcus Leipziger, Consulting Librarian. 3

HISTORY.—Founded 1886; support, public moneys; income for 1900, $44,000. 3 Branches: 113 East 59th Street, founded 1886; 106 Avenue C, founded 1887; 174 East 110th Street, founded 1896. Librarian's office, 113 East 59th Street.

REGULATIONS.—Open 9 A.M.–9 P.M.; reference and circulating; privileges free.

RESOURCES.—76,779 vols. Main Library, 28,271 vols.: including *Biography*, 2613 vols.; *Musical scores;* complete file of *New York Herald; Hebrew*, 720 vols.; *Russian*, 1049 vols. Branches: 59th Street Branch, 22,178 vols., including *Hebraica*, 675 vols.; Avenue C Branch, 9,445 vols.; 110th Street Branch, 14,912 vols.; travelling libraries department, 9,445 vols.

* **All Saints Academy School of Manhattan,** 1967 Madison Avenue, New York City. Sister M. Quigley, in charge. 4

HISTORY.—Founded 1882.

REGULATIONS.—Open 180 days in the year; 5 hours each week for circulation; free to limited class.

RESOURCES.—620 vols.

American Bible Society Library. 5000 vols. Transferred to New York Public Library; Astor, Lenox, and Tilden Foundations, *q.v.*

* **American Chemical Society Library,** 108 West 55th Street, New York City. 5

HISTORY.—Founded 1876; supported by Society; income for 1900, $500.

REGULATIONS.—Reference library; privileges free.

RESOURCES.—5000 vols.; entirely scientific.

American Ethnological Society Library. *See* American Museum of Natural History.

American Female Guardian Society, 29 East 29th Street, New York City. Miss J. L. Wood, Principal of "Home" School. 6

HISTORY.—Founded 1872; 13 school libraries; mostly gifts. Historical notice in "Our Golden Jubilee," 1854.

RESOURCES.—About 3000 vols., mostly supplementary readers, histories, geographies, and other school books.

American Geographical Society, 15 W. 81st Street, New York City. George C. Hurlbut, Librarian. 7

HISTORY.—Founded 1852; income for 1900, $1500. Historical notice in "Public Libraries in the U. S. A." (Wash., 1876), p. 356, 939–941.

REGULATIONS.—Open 10 A. M.–5 P. M.; reference only; privileges obtained by joining the Society.

RESOURCES.—About 30,000 vols. and 6000 pamphlets; consisting of geographical works, *Voyages*, *Travels*, and *Transactions and Bulletins of Geographical Societies*, *Atlases* of seventeenth and eighteenth centuries, and *Charts*, principally of United States Government.

* **American Hebrew Library,** Whitestone, Long Island, N. Y. Harry Levin, in charge. 8

HISTORY.—Founded 1898; free to the public; association library; supported by State aid and gifts; income for 1900, $143.94.

REGULATIONS.—Open 240 days in the year; 8 hours each week for reference and circulation.

RESOURCES.—334 vols.

American Institute Library, 19 and 21 West 44th Street, New York City. George Whitefield, Jr., Clerk. 9

HISTORY.—Founded 1829; association library; supported by the Institute; expenditures for 1900, $1562.80. Historical notice in "Public Libraries in the U. S. A." (Wash., 1876), p. 938–939.

REGULATIONS.—Open 9 A. M.–6 P. M.; membership to Institute and Library $10 initiation fee and $5 a year.

RESOURCES.—14,278 vols.; for many years its purchases have been confined to works on *Agriculture*, *Chemistry*, and the *Industrial Arts*.

American Institute of Electrical Engineers, Room 1004, 26 Cortlandt Street, New York City. Miss Josephine T. Bragg, Librarian. 10

HISTORY.—Founded 1884; society library; supported by the Institute.

American Institute of Electrical Engineers (*continued*).

REGULATIONS.— Open 9 A. M.-6 P. M.; free to the public for reference only on application to the librarian. Historical notices in "New York Times (Saturday Review)," November 9, 1901; "Electrical World and Engineer," May 25, 1901; and "The Engineer" (London), April 19, 1901.

RESOURCES.—8000 vols. and 1400 pamphlets; works on *Electricity* exclusively.

* **American Jewish Historical Society,** 736 Lexington Avenue, New York City. 11

Organized June 5, 1892; "its object is the collection, preservation, and publication of material having reference to the history of the Jews on the American continent." The Society owns a number of books, manuscripts, and portraits.

American Museum of Natural History, 77th Street and Central Park West, New York City. Anthony Woodward, Ph.D., Librarian. 12

HISTORY.—Founded 1869; free to the public; supported by endowments. The American Ethnological Library is now, virtually, a part of this Library. It has been deposited with it for about a year, and will be incorporated with it. It is included in this report.

REGULATIONS.—Open 9 A. M.-5 P. M., for reference only.

RESOURCES.—53,000 vols. of scientific works. Specialties: *Scientific Periodicals;* the D. G. Elliott Library of *Ornithology;* the J. C. Jay Library of *Conchology*, 1273 vols., and the Frederick A. Constable Library of *Conchology* of 250 vols.; the J. Carson Brevoort Library of *Herpetology, Ichthyology,* and *Marine Zoölogy;* the H. Edwards Library of *Entomology;* the Jules Marcou Library of *Geology, Palæontology,* and *Mineralogy;* the Hon. H. J. Jewett Library of *Early Voyages and Travels;* and the Halstead Library of *Recent Voyages and Travels;* 638 *Geological Maps* of North and South America; Library of the American Ethnological Society, founded in 1844, 750 vols. and about 300 pamphlets. For history of this library, see "Public Libraries in the U. S. A." (Wash., 1876), p. 355-356. The Library of the Ecumenical Council, held in New York in 1900, consisting of 3166 vols., 31 maps, and numerous pamphlets, has been permanently deposited here. This is a General Missionary Library, consisting of works about missions, as well as those written by missionaries, and is to be kept separate from the general library.

American Numismatic and Archæological Society, 17 West 43d Street (Academy of Medicine Building), New York City. Herbert Valentine, Librarian. 13

HISTORY.—Founded April 6, 1858; supported by endowment and dues. Historical notices in Proceedings, 1888–92, and in "Public Libraries in the U. S. A." (Wash., 1876), p. 356.

REGULATIONS.—Open Thursday evenings and on nights of regular and special meetings; reference; privileges extended to members of Society.

RESOURCES.—2500 vols. and 10,000 pamphlets, largely numismatic; the rest are mainly archæological.

American Seamen's Friend Society, 76 Wall Street, New York City. W. C. Stitt, Secretary. 14

HISTORY.—Founded 1858; free loan or travelling libraries; supported by gifts. Up to April 1, 1900, the Society had sent out 10,717 new libraries of about 43 vols. each, containing 582,727 vols., with 12,672 reshipments, accessible to 412,115 seamen. These libraries are placed aboard merchantmen and U. S. naval vessels, and in naval hospitals and life-saving stations. These libraries contain books of biography, travel and adventures, popular science, history, fiction, and religion. In each library go a Bible, atlas, dictionary, and several books in German, Danish, Swedish, and some other language.

American Society for the Prevention of Cruelty to Animals, Madison Avenue and 26th Street, New York City. John P. Haines, President. 15

HISTORY.—Founded 1866.

REGULATIONS.—Reference library for the exclusive use of the Society

RESOURCES.—3000 vols. and about 4000 pamphlets.

American Society of Civil Engineers, 220 West 57th Street, New York City. Charles Warren Hunt, Secretary. 16

HISTORY.—Founded 1852.

REGULATIONS.—Open 9 A. M.–10 P. M., except Sundays and holidays; for reference only; "free to any well-behaved seeker for information."

American Society of Civil Engineers (*continued*).

RESOURCES.—11,417 vols. and 20,476 pamphlets on *Civil Engineering*. A printed catalogue of 700 pages has recently been published.

American Veterinary College. *See* New York American Veterinary College Library.

Apprentices' Library. *See* General Society of Mechanics and Tradesmen of the City of New York.

Architects, American Institute of. *See* New York Chapter of the American Institute of Architects,

* **Arion Club Library,** 59th Street and Park Avenue, New York City. J. Bohne, Library Committee. 17

HISTORY.—Founded 1887; society library; supported by the Club.

REGULATIONS.—Reference and circulating; free to public for reference.

RESOURCES —2000 vols. and 50 pamphlets.

Art Students' League of New York, 215 West 57th Street, New York City. Harriet F. Clark, Chairman of the Library Committee. 18

HISTORY.—Founded 1875.

REGULATIONS.—Open 8.30 A.M.–10 P.M.; reference and circulating; privileges extended to members of the League.

RESOURCES.—700 vols. Devoted entirely to *Art. Bound Periodicals*, 274 vols.; 14 *Art Periodicals* received monthly.

* **Arthur W. Tams Music Library,** 109 West 28th Street, New York City. Arthur W. Tams, Proprietor. 19

HISTORY.—Founded 1885; subscription library; income for 1900, $25,000.

REGULATIONS.—Reference and circulating; privileges secured by subscription.

RESOURCES.—Estimated at 500,000 vols. and 1,000,000 pamphlets.

Arthur Winter Memorial Library, in Staten Island Academy and Latin School, New Brighton, S. I., N. Y. Miss Marion Canfield, Librarian. 20

HISTORY.—Founded 1886; day-school library; supported by gifts.

REGULATIONS.—Open school days 8.40 A. M.-2.30 P. M.; Wednesdays until 5 P. M.; reference and circulating; privileges: circulation free; reference by letter of introduction.

RESOURCES.—8816 vols; especially designed for reference work in connection with the Academy in whose building it has its room.

* **Asacog Club Library,** 55 Hicks Street, Brooklyn, N. Y. Sarah Seaman, in charge. 21

HISTORY.—Founded 1896; free to the public; income for 1900, $123.

REGULATIONS.—Open 118 days in the year; 4 hours each week for reference and circulation.

RESOURCES.—877 vols.

Aschenbroedel-Verein Library, 146 East 86th Street, New York City. Robert Reitz, Librarian. 22

HISTORY.—Founded 1865; society library; supported by the Verein

REGULATIONS.—Open 11 A.M.-3 P.M.; reference library; privileges secured by membership in the Club.

RESOURCES.—2500 vols.

Association of the Bar of the City of New York. *See* Bar Association of the City of New York.

Astor Library. *See* New York Public Library; Astor, Lenox, and Tilden Foundations.

Astoria Branch, Queens Borough Library. *See* Queens Borough Library.

Astral Branch. *See* Brooklyn Public Library.

Authors Club, Carnegie Building, Seventh Avenue and 56th Street, New York City. John D. Champlin, Library Committee. 23

HISTORY.—Organized 1882.

Authors Club (*continued*).

RESOURCES.—The Authors Club Library is divided into three sections: (1) Books written by members, about 1000 vols.; (2) Books of reference; (3) Library of *Literary Biography*, begun 1896, 1000 vols.

Bar Association of the City of New York, 42 West 44th Street, New York City. William Fargo Kip, Librarian. 24

HISTORY.—Founded 1870; private association library; supported by dues; has John E. Burrill Fund of $10,000 and John E. Parson Fund of $10,000; income for 1900, $86,145. Historical notice in "Public Libraries of the U. S. A." (Wash., 1876), p. 944-945.

REGULATIONS.—Open 9 A.M.-12 P.M.; reference and circulating; privileges enjoyed by members only.

RESOURCES.—52,154 vols. and 3107 pamphlets; special features, *Law* books.

Barnard College, Broadway and 120th Street, near Riverside Drive, New York City. Miss Mary Brown Sumner, Librarian. 25

Has no library to speak of (about 1550 vols.). Students enjoy full privileges of Columbia University Library.

Barnard School Library, 117 and 119 West 125th Street, New York City. Theodore E. Lyon, B.S., Librarian. 26

HISTORY.—Founded 1896; school library; supported by the School.

REGULATIONS.—Reference; for use of scholars and teachers only; privileges secured by applying to the Headmaster.

RESOURCES —5000 vols.

Bay Ridge Branch, Brooklyn Public Library. *See* Brooklyn Public Library.

HISTORY.—Formerly an independent library; founded in 1888, it was received into the Brooklyn Public Library, January 1, 1901.

Beachonian Society. *See* Eclectic College Library.

Bedford Branch, Brooklyn Public Library. *See* Brooklyn Public Library.

Bedford Park Branch, Brooklyn Public Library. *See* Brooklyn Public Library.

* **Bedford Park Club Library,** New York City. 27

History.—Founded 1897.

Regulations.—Free to club members.

* **Benjamin and Townsend Library,** Bellevue Hospital, East 26th Street and East River, New York City. Louis H. Brown, Librarian. 28

History.—Founded 1889.

Regulations.—Open 9 A.M.–5 P.M., Saturdays, 9 A.M.–12 M.

Resources.—About 4000 vols.

Berkeley Institute, 183–185 Lincoln Place, Brooklyn, N. Y. Miss Mary Francis, Secretary. 29

History.—Founded 1886; income, 1900, $200.

Regulations.—Open from 9 A.M.–5 P.M. every school day; reference and circulating; privileges obtained by Library Club membership and school tuition.

Resources.—About 3000 vols. and 200 pamphlets.

Berkeley School; Rosener Library, 435 Madison Avenue, New York City. J. Clark Read, Secretary. 30

History.—Founded 1894; private school library; printed catalogue.

Regulations.—Open during school hours; reference and circulating; privileges granted to members of the school.

Resources.—1500 vols.

Bethany Memorial Free Circulating Library, 1098 First Avenue, cor. East 60th Street, New York City. Gertrude S. Crockett, Librarian. 31

History.—Founded 1899; subscription library; free to public; supported by dues.

Regulations.—Open 11 A.M.–5 P.M.; Tuesdays, 2–6 and 7–9 P.M.; reference and circulating; privileges secured by signing application and giving suitable reference.

Resources.—About 1628 vols.

Bible Society, American. *See* New York Public Library; Astor, Lenox, and Tilden Foundations.

* **Bibliothek des Deutschen Liederkranz,** 115 East 58th Street, New York City. G. Otto Wolkwitz, Librarian. 32

HISTORY.—Founded 1868; society library; supported by the Society; income for 1900, $1050.

REGULATIONS.—Reference and circulating; free to public.

RESOURCES.—7000 vols.

Blackwell's Island Penitentiary Library, Blackwell's Island, New York City. John J. Fallon, Warden. 33

HISTORY.—Public library.

REGULATIONS.—Open 8.30 A.M.–5.30 P.M.; for prisoners and keepers.

RESOURCES.—2000 vols.

Blind, Free Circulating Library for the. *See* New York Free Circulating Library for the Blind.

Bloomingdale Branch, New York Public Library. *See* New York Public Library; Astor, Lenox, and Tilden Foundations.

Bnai Brith. *See* Maimonides Library.

Bnei Zion Library, 244 East Broadway, New York City. Abraham H. Brill, Librarian. 34

HISTORY.—Founded 1880; association library; supported by endowment; income for 1900, $400; has funds for the purchase of special collections.

REGULATIONS.—Open 7–10.30 P.M.; 1–6 P.M. on Saturdays and Sundays; reference and circulating; free to the public for reference; circulation restricted to members of the Bnei Zion Association.

RESOURCES.—About 1500 vols.; new books donated by individual members of the Association; the library contains "many hundreds of volumes" of *Hebrew Literature*, in the Hebrew, German, Russian, and English languages; many of the Hebrew books are very rare and old, a few of which are manuscripts in the handwriting of the authors.

Board of Foreign Missions of the Presbyterian Church. *See* Foreign Missions Library.

Bond Street Branch, New York Public Library. *See* New York Public Library; Astor, Lenox, and Tilden Foundations.

Booklovers Library, 29 West 33d Street, New York City, Edward J. Boyd, Librarian, *and* 198 Joralemon Street, Brooklyn, N. Y. 35

HISTORY.—Founded March, 1900; subscription library; delivers and collects books at the members' residences.

REGULATIONS.—Open 9 A. M.–5 P. M.; reference and circulating privileges secured by addressing Seymour Eaton, Librarian, 1323 Walnut Street, Philadelphia.

RESOURCES.—300,000 vols.

Borough of Queens Library, School No. 72, Maspeth, Borough of Queens, L. I., N. Y. Robert Eadie, Principal. 36

HISTORY.—School library; supported by taxation; income for 1900 about $60; free to the public.

REGULATIONS.—Open 9 A. M.–3 P. M.; reference and circulating; for use of teachers and pupils.

RESOURCES.—1363 vols. and 50 pamphlets.

Borough of Queens Library. *See also* Queens Borough Library.

Botanical Garden Library. *See* New York Botanical Garden.

Boys' and Girls' High School Library, Peter Cooper High School, 3080 Third Avenue, 157th Street and Third Avenue, New York City. Irving A. Heikes, Chairman Library Committee. 37

HISTORY—Founded 1897; school library; supported by taxation. Has Branches at 173d Street and Third Avenue, and at 144th Street and Mott Avenue.

Boys' and Girls' High School Library (*continued*).

REGULATIONS.—Reference and circulating; free to pupils of the school.
RESOURCES.—2400 vols.

Boys' Free Reading Room, 112 University Place, New York City. Miss Margaret J. Gibson, Librarian. 38

HISTORY.—Founded 1882; club library; supported by dues and voluntary contributions; has funds for purchase of special collections.

REGULATIONS.—Open 7–9.30 P.M.; reference and circulating; privileges secured by indorsement of parent or guardian.

RESOURCES.—780 vols.

Boys' High School Library, Marcy and Putnam Avenues, Brooklyn, N. Y. Daniel O'Connell Walsh, Librarian. 39

HISTORY.—Founded 1893; public school library.

REGULATIONS.—Open 8.45 A.M.–5 P.M. on school days; Saturdays, 9 A.M.–12 noon; reference; privileges extended to teachers and students of school only.

RESOURCES.—5100 vols. and 250 pamphlets; *English* and *American Literature*, 1000 vols.; *German*, 400 vols.; *French*, 200; *Greek* and *Latin*, 200 vols.

* **Boys' High School Library,** 60 West 13th Street, New York City. Hiram H. Bice, Librarian. 40

HISTORY.—Founded 1897; school library; supported by taxation; income for 1900, $254.

REGULATIONS.—Open 200 days in the year; 22½ hours each week for circulation; reference and circulating.

RESOURCES.—1570 vols. and 25 pamphlets.

Boys' Library. *See* House of Refuge, Randall's Island.

* **Brearley School Library,** 17 West 44th Street, New York City. F. G. Croswell, Librarian. 41

HISTORY.—School library; supported by the School.

REGULATIONS.—Reference and circulating; free to public.

RESOURCES.—5000 vols.

Bronx Botanical Garden Library. *See* New York Botanical Garden.

* **Bronx Free Library,** Washington Avenue and 176th Street, New York City. Miss J. Ida Bedell, Librarian. 42

HISTORY.—Founded Jan. 5, 1901; free public library; supported by public money and subscriptions for annual membership (dues, $5).

REGULATIONS.—Open Mondays and Thursdays 9 A.M.–12 M., Tuesdays and Fridays, 2–5 P.M., Wednesdays and Saturdays, 6.30–9.30 P.M., except legal holidays; reference and circulating; privileges secured on application with acceptable guarantor.

RESOURCES.—About 2200 vols. and 200 pamphlets.

Brooklyn College of Pharmacy, 329 Franklin Avenue, Brooklyn, N. Y. Dr. Charles H. Meyer, Librarian. 43

HISTORY.—Founded 1891; college library; supported by dues; income, 1900, $300, from Kings County Pharmaceutical Society; annual commencement contains historical notice.

REGULATIONS.—Open 9 A.M.–6 P.M., September to June; reference; privileges enjoyed by members of Kings County Pharmaceutical Society, students of College, and members of the College Alumni Association.

RESOURCES.—1800 vols. and 2100 pamphlets; specialties, *Pharmacy*, 800 vols., *Chemistry*, 400 vols., and *Botany*, 250 vols.

Brooklyn Directory Library, 317 Washington Street, Brooklyn, N. Y. George Upington, Publisher. 44

HISTORY.—Private library; supported by reference fees; copying done at moderate rates.

REGULATIONS.—Open 8 A.M.–6 P.M.; reference only.

RESOURCES.—*Brooklyn Directories* from 1834 to date, and 250 out-of-town directories, embracing those of all the important cities, towns, and states in the Union, including a file of the New York City Directory from 1827 to date. Catalogues furnished on application.

Brooklyn Institute of Arts and Sciences; Children's Museum Library, 185 Brooklyn Avenue, Brooklyn, N. Y. Miss Miriam S. Draper, Librarian. 45

Brooklyn Institute of Arts and Sciences (*continued*)

HISTORY.—Opened April, 1900; free to public; supported by public moneys and endowment; income for books, 1900, $750.

REGULATIONS.—Open 9 A.M.–6 P.M.; reference; entirely free.

RESOURCES.—1200 vols. and 300 pamphlets; scientific and historical reference library.

Brooklyn Institute of Arts and Sciences; Department Libraries, Eastern Parkway and Washington Avenue, Brooklyn, N. Y. Miss Susan A. Hutchinson, Librarian. 46

HISTORY.—Founded 1824; free library; supported by public moneys and gifts. The library has been in storage for several years until February 1, 1900. It is being reorganized, but is not yet fully open. Historical notice in "Public Libraries in the U. S. A." (Wash., 1876), p. 881.

REGULATIONS.—Open 9 A.M.–6 P.M.; reference; privileges obtained on application.

RESOURCES.—About 24,000 vols. and several thousand pamphlets. It is proposed to specialize in the *Sciences* and *Arts*, supplementing the Museum collections.

Brooklyn Law Library. *See* Law Library, Brooklyn.

Brooklyn Library, 197 Montague Street, Brooklyn, N. Y. Charles Edward Farrington, Acting Librarian. 47

HISTORY.—Established 1857; subscription library; supported partly by endowment, partly by dues ($5.00 a year); income, 1900, about $21,000. This library has branch stations at 981 and 1167 Fulton Street, 19 Greene Avenue, 570 Bedford Avenue, 796 Flatbush Avenue, and at Flatbush Avenue, cor. of Seventh Street. Cary Fund, $5000, income for books in higher classes. Historical notices have been printed in local newspapers; "Public Libraries in the U. S. A." (Wash., 1876), p. 878–881 and Brooklyn Eagle's "History of the City of Brooklyn," vol. 2, p. 772–773.

REGULATIONS.—Open 8.30 A.M.–9 P.M.; reference and circulating; privileges may be obtained by becoming a Permanent member for $500; a Life member, $100; or Annual member, $5.00; have interchanged with other libraries at times on application.

RESOURCES.—152,474 vols. and 19,000 pamphlets. Special features —*Biography, History, Travels, etc.*, 36,644 vols.; *Collective Works, Periodicals, etc.*, 13,346 vols.; *Foreign Languages*, works not elsewhere classified, 10,736 vols.; *Philosophy, Education, Fine Arts*, 10,234 vols.; *Poetry, Drama. Essays, etc.*, 9242 vols.; *Religion* and *Theology*, 8710 vols.; *Sciences* and *Useful Arts*, 14,955 vols.; *Other Classes* and *Fiction*, 34,928 vols.; Unclassified, 5560 vols. The Library owns the James A. H. Bell Library of 10,425 vols., which is kept separate from the main library. It has a separate catalogue, compiled by Mr. Bell, bound in 69 royal octavo volumes.

Brooklyn Public Library, Bedford Branch (and Offices of General Administration), 26 Brevoort Place, Brooklyn, N. Y. Frank Pierce Hill, Librarian. 48

HISTORY.—Authorized by Act of Legislature, May 3, 1892; opened December, 1897; free public library; income for 1900, $40,000; 1901, $100,000. The Library has the following Branches: WILLIAMSBURG BRANCH, 474 Bedford Ave., founded 1899, 9740 vols., including those of the former Eastern District School Library; EAST BRANCH, 29 Pennsylvania Ave., founded 1899, 4634 vols.; SOUTH BROOKLYN BRANCH, 1147 Fourth Ave., founded 1899, 4508 vols.; FLATBUSH BRANCH, 5 Caton Ave., founded February 21, 1899, received as a branch January 1, 1900, 4810 vols.; PROSPECT BRANCH, 372 Ninth St., founded 1900, 1628 vols.; BEDFORD PARK BRANCH, 185 Brooklyn Ave., founded 1898, 2851 vols.; SCHERMERHORN STREET BRANCH (formerly Free Lending Library of the Union for Christian Work), 67 Schermerhorn St., founded 1882, received as a branch January 1, 1901, 46,000 vols.; BAY RIDGE BRANCH, Second Ave. and 73d St., founded 1888, received as a branch January 1, 1901, 6197 vols.; FORT HAMILTON BRANCH, Fourth Ave. and 95th St., founded 1893, received as a branch January 1, 1901, 6600 vols.; NEW UTRECHT BRANCH, Eighteenth and Benson Aves., Bath Beach, founded February 28, 1895, received as a branch January 1, 1901, 3600 vols.; CITY PARK BRANCH, 186 Bridge St., founded 1901, 1800 vols.; CARROLL PARK BRANCH, 322 Smith St., founded 1901, 1200 vols.; BUSHWICK BRANCH, 198 Montrose Ave., founded 1901, 1200 vols.; SARATOGA BRANCH, 1035 Putnam Ave., founded 1901, 500 vols.; TOMPKINS PARK BRANCH, Tompkins Park, founded 1896, received as a branch 1901, 2000 vols.; ASTRAL BRANCH, Franklin and Java Sts., founded 1888, received as a branch September 15, 1901, 7067 vols.; TRAVELLING LIBRARIES DEPARTMENT, founded 1899.

Brooklyn Public Library (*continued*).
Historical notice in Handbook for 1900.

Regulations.—Open 9 A.M.–9 P.M., Sundays, 2–6 P.M.; reference and circulating; privileges obtained by giving name of a responsible citizen as a guarantor; sometimes interchanges with other libraries.

Resources.—120,000 vols.

Brooklyn Public Library Association, Brooklyn, N. Y. Mrs. Mary E. Cragie, President.

History.—This is an association of Brooklyn men and women for the promotion of library progress. It was instrumental in founding the Brooklyn Public Library, which it operated until that institution was turned over to the city authorities. It also aided in establishing as independent libraries the Flatbush Free Library and the Tompkins Park Free Library, both now branches of the Brooklyn Public Library. The Association does not now operate libraries.

Brooklyn Society of the New Church. *See* Free Library and Reading Room of the Brooklyn Society of the New Church.

Brooklyn Young Men's Christian Association Library, 502 Fulton Street, cor. Bond Street, Brooklyn, N. Y. Miss Irene A. Hackett, Librarian. 49

History.—Founded 1853; institutional library; supported by annual appropriation from endowment and dues; income for 1900, $2420. The library has the following branches: Bedford Branch, 416–420 Gates Ave., founded 1891, 1400 vols., of which 100 vols relate to *Bible Study;* East New York Branch, Pennsylvania and Liberty Avenues, 400 vols.; Eastern District Branch, 131 South 8th Street, 300 vols., 230 vols in Boy's Department; Long Island College Branch, Henry and Pacific Streets, 200 vols.; and Prospect Park Branch, 357–365 Ninth Street, founded October 1, 1891, 500 vols., including "Louis V. B. Bennett Memorial Reference Library" of 205 vols.; 275 vols. in Boy's Department. Historical notice in Regents' Annual Report.

Regulations.—Open 8.30 A.M.–10 P.M., except Sundays; reference and circulating; privileges granted to members of the Association only.

RESOURCES.—About 18,000 vols. and 2000 pamphlets. Specialties: 500 vols. of best and latest books for *Bible Study* and over 2000 vols. of *Periodicals* indexed in Poole.

Broome Street Free Library and Reading-Room, 395 Broome Street, New York City. Horace E. Waste, Librarian. 50

HISTORY.—Founded 1885; free public library; under control of the New York City Mission and Tract Society, which is supported by voluntary contributions.

REGULATIONS.—Open 4–9 P.M., Tuesdays, Wednesdays, and Fridays; reference and circulating; privileges may be obtained upon giving satisfactory references.

RESOURCES.—About 2300 vols. and 13 pamphlets.

Bruce Branch, George; New York Public Library. *See* New York Public Library; Astor, Lenox, and Tilden Foundations.

Bryson Library of the Teachers College of the City of New York, West 120th Street, Morningside Heights, near Amsterdam Avenue, New York City. Miss Elizabeth G. Baldwin, Librarian. 51

HISTORY.—Founded 1887; university library; supported by endowment.

REGULATIONS.—Open 8.45 A.M.–5.45 P.M. daily, Saturdays, 9 A.M.–1 P.M.; reference and circulating; privileges enjoyed by registered students of Columbia University, Barnard College, Teachers College, and by all teachers in New York City; interchanges books with other libraries.

RESOURCES.—15,500 vols., mainly devoted to *Pedagogy*.

Bushwick Branch, Brooklyn Public Library. *See* Brooklyn Public Library.

Carroll Park Branch, Brooklyn Public Library. *See* Brooklyn Public Library.

Cathedral Free Circulating Library, Central Library, 536 Amsterdam Avenue, cor. 86th Street, New York City. Rev. Joseph H. McMahon, Ph.D., Director. 52

Cathedral Free Circulating Library (*continued*).

HISTORY.—Founded November, 1888; free public library; supported by public moneys and by the Cathedral corporation; income 1900, $13,050. This library has 11 Branches: BRANCH A, 44 Second Ave., founded 1891, 3500 vols.; BRANCH B, 420 East 80th St., founded 1892, 2500 vols.; BRANCH C, 147 East 43d St., founded 1894, 1300 vols.; BRANCH E, Tremont, founded 1896, 700 vols.; BRANCH F, 420 East 69th St., founded 1898, 4000 vols.; BRANCH G, 113 East 85th St., founded 1899, 3000 vols.; BRANCH H, 60th St. and 10th Ave., founded 1900, 700 vols.; BRANCH I, Monroe Ave. and Kingsbridge Road, founded 1901, 400 vols.; SACRED HEART BRANCH, 463 West 51st St., founded 1901, 5000 vols.; SAINT RAPHAEL BRANCH, 501 West 40th St., founded 1901, 3000 vols.; HOLY TRINITY BRANCH, 201 West 82d St., founded 1901, 1700 vols; ——— BRANCH, 123 East 50th St. Historical notice in "Messenger of the Sacred Heart, N. Y.," vol. 8 (1893), p. 887.

REGULATIONS.—Open 9 A. M.–9 P. M., except during the months of July and August; Sundays, 10 A. M.–12 P. M.; reference and circulating; privileges granted on presentation of name of any citizen as guarantor; interchanges with other libraries whenever asked.

RESOURCES.—Main Library, 52,890 vols. and about 2000 pamphlets; Branch libraries, 25,800 vols. The main library has a very complete collection of books in every department of *Roman Catholic Theology, Literature, and History,* in all about 6000 vols. There are also upwards of 700 vols. on *Music*, the nucleus of which was the collection of the late John R. G. Hassard, musical critic of the "New York Tribune." It also possesses many *Roman Catholic Periodicals* (English, French, Italian, Polish, and German) that are apparently not taken by any other public library.

* **Catherine Mission Library,** 201 South Street, New York City. Margaret A. Delany, Superintendent. 53

REGULATIONS.—Open 9 A.M.–7 P.M., except Sundays and holidays.

Catholic Club Library, 120 West 59th Street, New York City. James M. Mooney, Librarian. 54

HISTORY.—Founded 1871; supported by appropriation from funds of the Catholic Club. Catalogue published 1896.

REGULATIONS.—Open for use of members at all hours, and to ladies or representatives of members' families daily, except Sundays, between 2 and 5 P. M.; reference and circulating; privileges enjoyed by members.

RESOURCES.—35,000 vols.

Catholic Historical Society, 101 Greene Avenue, Brooklyn, N. Y. Mark F. Vallette, President.

Century Association Library, 7 West 43d Street, New York City. Joseph Herbert Senter, Librarian. 55

HISTORY.—Founded 1847; society library; supported by the Association; income for 1900, $3500. Has fund of $2000 for purchase of periodicals.

REGULATIONS.—Open 8 A.M.–2 o'clock of the next A.M.; reference library; privileges secured by membership in Association or an introduction through a member.

RESOURCES.—12,500 vols. and 800 pamphlets. This library has a set of 68 vols. of *Journal des Scavans*, 1665–1720; a nearly complete set of the *Mercure de France*, 1633–1819; and many art works. It also has numerous works on *New York and United States History*. A special feature is the *James Lorimer Graham Library* of about 4000 vols. of "the aristocracy of literature," including many rare *First Editions, Collections of Autographs and Extra-Illustrated Books*. A catalogue of this collection was published in 1896. A catalogue of the library was printed in 1879.

* **Chamber of Commerce of the State of New York,** 32 Nassau Street, New York City. George Wilson, Secretary. 56

HISTORY.—Founded 1858; corporation library; supported by the corporation.

REGULATIONS.—Reference library; privileges restricted to limited class.

RESOURCES.—6500 vols.

Charity Organization Society Library, 105 East 22d Street, New York City. Miss Mary Forbes, Librarian. 57

HISTORY.—Founded 1893; free public library for reference; supported by the Society and special contributions; no income except about $150 for purchase of books.

REGULATIONS.—Open 9 A.M.–5 P.M.; reference only; privileges granted on application to the Librarian; does not interchange with other libraries.

RESOURCES.—2100 vols., 1200 pamphlets. Collection consists entirely of books and pamphlets on *Practical Sociology*, i. e., *Charity, Pensions, Defectives, Charitable Institutions, etc.*

Chatham Square Branch, New York Public Library. *See* New York Public Library; Astor, Lenox, and Tilden Foundations.

Children's Museum Library of the Brooklyn Institute of Arts and Sciences. *See* Brooklyn Institute of Arts and Sciences.

Circulating Library of the College Settlement. *See* College Settlement Library.

City Library, 12 City Hall, New York City. Philip Baer, City Librarian. 58

History.—Founded 1847; supported by public money.

Regulations.—Open 10 A.M.–4 P.M., Saturdays 10 A.M.–12 M.; reference only; free to the public. It interchanges with other libraries; historical notice in "Public Libraries of the U. S. A." (Wash., 1876), p. 918–919.

Resources.—21,000 volumes. The City Library contains *Reports* from *National, State, and City Governments; Proceedings of the Common Council* from 1647 to date; *City Directories* from 1795 to date; *Municipal Reports* from all the large cities of this country, and many foreign reports; and also much miscellaneous matter of a *Statistical* nature.

* **City Mission and Tract Society Library,** United Charities Building, Fourth Avenue and 22d Street, New York City.

City Park Branch, Brooklyn Public Library. *See* Brooklyn Public Library.

* **Clionian Society Library, College of the City of New York,** 105 East Broadway, New York City. J. C. Mackby, Librarian. 59

History.—Founded 1870; society library; income for 1900, $50.

Regulations.—Reference and circulating.

Resources.—1265 vols. and 59 pamphlets.

College for the Training of Teachers. *See* Bryson Library of the Teachers College.

College of Pharmacy of the City of New York, 115 West 68th Street, New York City. Orange J. Griffin, Assistant Secretary. 60

HISTORY.—Founded 1829; free to public.

REGULATIONS.—Open 10 A.M.–4 P.M., Saturdays 10 A.M.–12 M.; reference only; anyone of good personal appearance and with introduction may consult the library on personal application.

RESOURCES.—Estimated to be 8000 vols. and 12,000 pamphlets. The volumes are on *Chemistry, Pharmacy, Botany, Materia Medica, Physics, etc.*

College of Physicians and Surgeons, 437 West 59th Street, New York City. Edward T. Boag, Assistant Registrar. 61

"A few books of reference collected by the various departments, but they do not constitute a library."

College of St. Francis Xavier, Faculty Library, 30 West 16th Street, New York City. Rev. John F. O'Donovan, S. J., Librarian. 62

HISTORY.—Founded 1847; college library; supported by moneys given by the faculty.

REGULATIONS.—Privilege to consult Faculty Library may be obtained from the President of the College.

RESOURCES.—82,000 vols. Specialties: Entire collection of "*Jesuit Relations*"; entire collection of the Bollandists' "*Acta Sanctorum*" to date; files of *The Month, Dublin Review, American Catholic Quarterly Review,* and *American Ecclesiastical Review.*

College of St. Francis Xavier, Students' Library, 30 West 16th Street, New York City. Rev. John F. O'Donovan, S.J., Librarian. 63

HISTORY.—Founded 1847; college library; supported by dues from the students; income for 1900, $970.

REGULATIONS.—Open each afternoon from 2.30–3.30 P.M.; circulating library; privileges enjoyed by students of the College.

RESOURCES.—17,000 vols.

College of the City of New York, 17 Lexington Avenue, Charles George Herbermann, Librarian. 64

HISTORY.—Founded 1852; supported partly from public moneys and partly from endowment; income from endowments for purchase of books and periodicals for 1900, about $1500; brief historical notice in book catalogue, published in 1877, also in "Public Libraries of the U. S. A." (Wash., 1876), p. 945-946.

REGULATIONS.—Open 8.30 A.M.-4 P.M.; Saturdays 9.30 A.M.-12 M.; reference and circulating; the library privileges are enjoyed by the students and instructors of the College, its Alumni, and also by the teachers of the public schools; have rarely interchanged with other libraries, but would not object to do so.

RESOURCES.—33,647 vols., June 30, 1900, and 1471 pamphlets.

College Settlement Library, 95 Rivington Street, New York City. Miss Mabel H. Duncan, Librarian. 65

HISTORY.—Founded 1888; free public library; supported by gifts and from general funds of the Settlement.

REGULATIONS.—Open Wednesdays, 3.30-5 and 7.30-9 P.M., Fridays, 3.30-5 P.M., and Saturdays, 10 A.M.-12 M.; circulating library; privileges obtained on application and reference.

RESOURCES.—2400 vols.; general collection, largely for children; current magazines on reading table.

Colored Orphan Asylum, West 143d Street and Amsterdam Avenue. Gertrude Smith, Principal.

Reports no library. The few story books the children have were donated.

Columbia University in the City of New York, Morningside Heights, West 116th Street and Amsterdam Avenue. James Hulme Canfield, LL.D., Librarian; Charles Alexander Nelson, A.M., Reference Librarian. 66

HISTORY.—Founded 1757; free to University officers and students and (within the building) to others properly introduced; supported by endowments and gifts. Historical notices—Edwards, Edw., "Memoirs of

Libraries" (Lond., 1859) vol. 2, p. 175–176; "Columbia College Library," by W. A. Jones, 1866; in *University Quarterly*, 1861, vol. 3, p. 41–61; "Public Libraries in the U. S. A." (Wash., 1876), p. 30, 104–5; Wilson, J. G., "Memorial History of the City of N. Y." (N. Y., 1893), vol. 4, p. 85–87; "The New Columbia," by C. Alex. Nelson, in *Lib. Journal*, 1897, vol. 22, p. 746–747, and in *Columbia University Bulletin*, Dec., 1897, no. 18, p. 35–38; by George H. Baker, in *Lib. Journal*, 1898, vol. 23, p. 103–106; by James H. Canfield, in *Columbia University Quarterly*, 1900, vol. 2, p. 101–107. Income for 1900 nearly $70,000.

REGULATIONS.—Open 8.30 A.M.–11 P.M. (Oct.–June), and to 10 P.M. (July–Sept.); reference and circulation to officers and students; reference only to all others; privileges freely extended to all who are properly introduced; interchanges with other libraries.

RESOURCES.—319,000 vols.; 40,000 pamphlets. Special funds for special collections. Among the specialties are:—*Law Library*, 30,000 vols.; *Avery Architectural Library*, 18,000 vols.; *Phœnix Collection*, 7000 vols.; *Sociology*, 5211 vols.; *Temple Emanu-el Library of Biblical and Rabbinical Literature*, 2500 vols., 1000 pamphlets and 50 mss.; *Music*, 1200 vols.; *Goethe Collection*, 1153 vols.; *Shakespeare Collection*, 967 vols.; *Kant Collection*, 787 vols.; *Garden Library of Southern Americana*, 994 vols.; *Mary Queen of Scots Collection*, 521 vols.; *Holland Society*, 500 vols.; Works on *Education* in the University and Teachers College Libraries as per printed catalogue, about 13,500 titles. In addition to these there are a number of laboratory libraries.

Columbian Reading Union, Paulist Parish Library, 415 West 59th Street, New York City. Rev. Thomas McMillan, Director. Reached by Sunday School entrance from Columbus Avenue, near 59th Street. 67

HISTORY.—Founded September, 1860; supported by voluntary gifts; income for 1900, $250; the library is managed by a committee of young people under the supervision of the Director.

REGULATIONS.—Open 9 A.M.–12 M., Sundays; also Monday evenings and Wednesday afternoons and evenings; reference and circulating; privileges secured by application to the Director.

RESOURCES.—About 4000 vols. This is an organization for the diffusion of good literature, especially Roman Catholic literature. It has headquarters as above, and correspondents in various other cities.

Comstock School, 32 West 40th Street, New York City. Lydia Day, in charge. 68

REGULATIONS.—Reference library and reading-room for day and boarding pupils.

RESOURCES.—1000 vols.

Conrad Poppenhusen Association. *See* Poppenhusen Institute Library.

Cooper Union for the Advancement of Science and Art, in Cooper Institute, Eighth Street and 4th Avenue, New York City. L. C. Levin Jordan, Assistant Secretary. 69

HISTORY.—Incorporated 1857; free to public; supported by endowment; and from the general fund of the Institution. Historical notice—"Public Libraries in the U. S. A." (Wash., 1876), p. 943-944.

REGULATIONS.—Open 8 A. M.-10 P. M.; Sundays, October to May, 12 M.-9 P. M.; reference library; can be used by any respectable person over 14 years of age.

RESOURCES.—About 37,000 vols.; has a good collection of *Pictures, portraits, maps, etc.*, relating to the early history of *New York City*, which has been indexed; also a collection of *Ballads and Poetry* comprising 8000 titles, indexed; 435 *Periodicals* on file.

Cornell University Medical College, Department of Pathology Library, First Avenue and 28th Street, New York City. James Ewing, in charge. 70

HISTORY.—Founded 1899; college library; supported by University funds; income for 1900, $2500.

REGULATIONS.—Open 8 A. M.-6 P. M.; reference and circulating; open to attachés of Department and members of Faculty; would like to interchange books with other libraries.

RESOURCES.—About 2000 vols. and 4000 pamphlets; limited to works on *Pathology*. The 4000 pamphlets constituted the "Handapparat" of the late Prof. Birch-Hirschfeld. The library also possesses some very old Latin works on *Medicine*.

Corporation Counsel, Law Department Library, Staats-Zeitung Building, Tryon Row, New York City. James M. Valles, Librarian. 71

HISTORY.—Supported by the City of New York.

REGULATIONS.—Open 10 A. M.–5 P. M.; use strictly restricted to the Corporation Counsel and his Assistants.

RESOURCES.—About 6000 vols.

Cummings Library, 21 Coenties Slip, New York City. I. Maguire, Librarian. 72

HISTORY.—Founded 1874; supported by the Protestant Episcopal Seamen's Society; out-door station.

REGULATIONS.—Open 8.30 A. M.–10 P. M.; reference; the library and reading-room are open to all sailors and boatmen.

RESOURCES.—1500 vols.

De La Salle Institute, 106 and 108 West 59th Street, New York City. B. P. Blimond, Librarian. 73

HISTORY.—Founded 1848; school library.

REGULATIONS.—Reference.

RESOURCES.—About 5000 vols. and 1000 pamphlets; leading features are *Ancient Classical Literature, General Science,* and *Engineering.*

Deaf and Dumb, Institution for the Instruction of the. *See* New York Institution for the Instruction of the Deaf and Dumb.

Department Libraries, Brooklyn Institute of Arts and Sciences. *See* Brooklyn Institute of Arts and Sciences. Department Libraries.

DeWitt Clinton High School Library, 74 West 102d Street, New York City. Hiram H. Bice, Librarian. 74

HISTORY.—Founded 1897; school library; supported by appropriations from the Board of Education.

REGULATIONS.—Open 9 A. M.–3.30 P. M.; reference and circulating; privileges obtained by pupils on application.

RESOURCES.—1650 vols.

De Witt Memorial Free Library, 286 Rivington Street, New York City. Malcolm R. Birnie, Librarian. 75

HISTORY.—Founded 1882; free to public; city mission supported by public moneys. Historical notice in "City Mission Monthly."

REGULATIONS.—Open 3–8 P.M. daily, except Sundays and holidays; reference and circulating; privileges secured on written application, with signature of a business man as reference.

RESOURCES.—2500 vols. and 40 pamphlets; nearly 600 vols. of books for the young.

Directory Libraries. *See* Trow Directory Library *and* Brooklyn Directory Library.

East Branch, Brooklyn Public Library. *See* Brooklyn Public Library.

East Side House Settlement Library. *See* Webster Free Library.

* **Eastern District School Library,** Brooklyn, N. Y. *See* Brooklyn Public Library; Williamsburg Branch.

HISTORY.—This library is now included in the Williamsburg Branch of the Brooklyn Public Library, at 380 Bedford Avenue.

Eclectic Medical College Library, 239 East 14th Street, New York City. George W. Boskowitz, Dean. 76

HISTORY.—Founded 1865.

REGULATIONS.—Open 9 A.M.–5 P.M.; reference library; privileges obtained by attendance upon the College.

RESOURCES.—2308 vols. and 12,880 pamphlets; medical library.

Editors' Library. *See* Methodist Library.

Educational Alliance Library. *See* Aguilar Free Library, 197 East Broadway.

Ely's (Misses) School for Girls, 340 West 86th Street, New York City. Miss Elizabeth L. Ely, Librarian. 77

HISTORY.—School library; supported by the School; strictly private, open only to members of the School.

REGULATIONS.—Reference and circulating.

RESOURCES.—About 1000 volumes.

* **English and Classical School for Girls,** 43 West 47th Street, New York City. 78

HISTORY.—School library; supported by the School.
REGULATIONS.—Reference and circulating; free to limited class.
RESOURCES.—About 2000 vols.

Equitable Insurance Library, 120 Broadway, New York City. Miss Mary Emily Miller, Librarian. 79

REGULATIONS.—Open 9 A. M.–4 P. M.; Saturdays, 9 A. M.–12 M.; reference; privileges extended to all persons interested in insurance.

RESOURCES.— 7000 vols.; contains the most complete collection of *Insurance Literature* ever brought together, and is thoroughly classified and catalogued. It contains the *Collection of* the late *Cornelius Walford*, consisting of some 3000–4000 vols., which is rich in insurance books of the sixteenth and seventeenth centuries. Complete sets of the *Insurance Reports* of twenty-two States, with more or less complete files from twenty-seven other States. Books relating to great *Fires, Storms, Wrecks, Plagues, Epidemics,* and *Earthquakes.*

Equitable Life Assurance Society; Law Library, 120 Broadway, New York City. Thomas Campbell, Librarian. 80

HISTORY.—Founded 1876; supported from general funds of the institution owning the library.

REGULATIONS.—Open 60 hours each week during 8 months, October to June, viz., 9 A. M.–7 P. M., except Sundays and holidays and 48 hours during 4 months, June to September, inclusive, viz., 9 A. M.–5 P. M.; reference; privileges may be secured by becoming a member of the Lawyers' Club or a tenant of the building.

RESOURCES.—17,165 vols.; its leading features are *Legal Treatises, Reports of Decisions, Digests of Reports, Collections of Cases, Statute Law, Periodicals, and Reference Books.*

Erasmus Hall High School Library, Flatbush Avenue, Brooklyn, N. Y. Mary A. Kingsbury, Librarian. 81

HISTORY.—Founded 1787; supported by public moneys.

REGULATIONS.—Open 8.30 A.M.–1 P.M., 2 P.M.–5 P.M.; reference and circulating; full privileges enjoyed by pupils and teachers of the School.

RESOURCES.—3500 vols.

Ethical Culture Schools Library, 109 West 54th Street, New York City. Matilde Kitzinger, Secretary. 82

REGULATIONS.—Open during school sessions from 9 A.M.–12 M.; reference and circulating; privileges enjoyed by pupils and teachers of the Schools.

RESOURCES.—4921 vols.; *Pedagogical* reference library and *Reading for Young.*

* **Father Malone Memorial Library,** Berry Street, near South 2d Street, Brooklyn, N. Y. 82a

REGULATIONS.—Free circulating library.

RESOURCES.—20,000 vols.

* **Female Academy of the Sacred Heart Library,** 130th Street, New York City. Ellen White, R.H.S., Librarian. 83

HISTORY.—Founded 1847; school library; supported by the Academy; income for 1900, $494.16.

REGULATIONS.—Open 365 days in the year; 16 hours each week for reference and 7 hours for circulation; free to a limited class.

RESOURCES.—5944 vols.

* **Female Institution of the Visitation,** Brooklyn, N. Y. Sister Mary Evangelista, in charge. 84

HISTORY.—Founded 1855; school library; supported by the Institution.

REGULATIONS.—Reference and circulating; free to a limited class.

RESOURCES.—3000 vols. and 500 pamphlets.

Fifth Avenue Library, 464 Fifth Avenue, Brooklyn, N. Y. Mrs. Louisa Ruger and Mrs. M. Frederick, Proprietors. 85

HISTORY.—Founded 1883; private circulating library; supported by subscriptions; income for 1900, $510.

REGULATIONS.—Open 9 A. M.–10 P. M.; circulating; dues, $3 a year, $1 for 3 months, or 40 cents a month.

RESOURCES.—5900 vols.

Five Points Mission Library and Free Reading-Room, 63 Park Street, Site of the Old Brewery, New York City. Rev. Aaron K. Sanford, Superintendent; John E. Parker, Librarian. 86

HISTORY.—Founded some 30 years ago; free to public; supported by voluntary contributions.

REGULATIONS.—Open evenings, 7.30–9 P. M.; reference; open to all who wish to read either books, papers, or pamphlets.

RESOURCES.—2100 vols.

Flatbush Branch, Brooklyn Public Library. *See* Brooklyn Public Library.

HISTORY.—Formerly an independent library, founded in 1899; it was received into the Brooklyn Public Library January 1, 1900.

Flushing High School Library. *See* High School Library, Flushing, L. I.

* **Flushing Institute Library,** Flushing, L. I., N. Y. E. A. Fairchild, Principal. 87

HISTORY.—Founded 1874; school library; free to a limited class; supported by the Institute.

REGULATIONS.—Reference and circulating.

RESOURCES.—1395 vols.

Flushing Library Association, Jamaica and Jaggar Avenues and Main Street, Flushing, L. I., N. Y. Miss Louise G. Hinsdale, Librarian. 88

HISTORY.—Founded 1858, incorporated 1869; free to the public; supported by public moneys; income for 1900, $3284.44.

REGULATIONS.—Open 9 A. M.–1 P. M., 3 P. M.–9 P. M., except Sundays and holidays; reference and circulating; privileges secured by registration.

RESOURCES.—About 6750 vols.

* **Flushing Seminary Library**, Flushing, L. I., N. Y. Miss Jeanette Pidgeon, Principal. 89

HISTORY.—School library; supported by Seminary; private reference library.

RESOURCES.—1404 vols.; use strictly limited to members of the school.

Foreign Missions Library, 156 Fifth Avenue, New York City. W. Henry Grant, Acting Librarian. 90

HISTORY.—Founded 1840; the property of the Board of Foreign Missions of the Presbyterian Church in the U. S. A., and supported from its funds; $1000 appropriated annually, the Acting Librarian serving gratuitously; brief notice of this library in "Memoirs of the Hon. Walter Lowrie," edited by his son.

REGULATIONS.—Open 9 A. M.–1 P. M., 2 P. M.–5 P. M., except Sundays and holidays, and Saturday afternoons during the summer months; reference and circulating; any student of missions is free to consult the files and borrow such books as are loaned.

RESOURCES.—7258 vols.; the library is designed for diffusing missionary information. It has a small museum connected with the library and a good collection of *Photographs*, *Lantern Slides*, and *Maps* in sheets. It has, also, numerous translations of the *Bible* and books in the *Chinese language* and about *China*.

Fort Hamilton Branch, Brooklyn Public Library. *See* Brooklyn Public Library.

HISTORY.—Formerly an independent library, founded in 1893; it was received into the Brooklyn Public Library, January 1, 1901.

* **Fortnightly Club Library,** 227 Warwick Street, Brooklyn, N. Y. 91

REGULATIONS.—Open Wednesday and Saturday afternoons and evenings.

Free Circulating Library. *See* New York Public Library; Astor, Lenox, and Tilden Foundations.

* **Free Circulating Library,** Clinton Avenue, New Brighton, S. I., N. Y.

Free Circulating Library for the Blind. *See* New York Free Circulating Library for the Blind.

Free Circulating Library of the West Side Settlement. *See* West Side Settlement, Young Women's Christian Association Free Circulating Library.

Free Lending Library of the Union for Christian Work, 67 Schermerhorn Street, Brooklyn, N. Y. *See* Brooklyn Public Library; Schermerhorn Street Branch.

Free Library. *See* DeWitt Memorial Free Library.

* **Free Library,** Astoria. *See* Queens Borough Library.

Free Library, College Point. *See* Borough of Queens Library.

Free Library and Reading—Room of the Brooklyn Society of the New Church, 98 South Elliott Place, Brooklyn, N. Y. Miss Elizabeth Tingle, Librarian. 92

HISTORY.—Founded about 1875; free library; partly supported by endowment of the Society; income for 1900 about $1100.

REGULATIONS.—Open 10 A. M.–12.30 P. M., 1.30 P. M.–6.30 P. M , and on Tuesdays, Thursdays, and Saturdays, 8–9 P. M.; reference and circulating; free on personal application.

RESOURCES.—About 2100 vols. and 100 pamphlets; especially devoted to *Swedenborg's Works and collateral literature.*

* **Free Library of St. Mark's Memorial Chapel,** 288 East 10th Street, New York City. Joseph S. Ruepp, Librarian. 93

HISTORY.—Founded 1883.

REGULATIONS.—Open 7–9 P. M. daily except Saturdays and Sundays.

RESOURCES.—About 1200 vols.

Free Library of the Five Points Mission. *See* Five Points Mission Library and Reading-Room.

Free Library of the General Society of Mechanics and Tradesmen of the City of New York. *See* General Society of Mechanics and Tradesmen of the City of New York.

Free School Library. *See* Union Free School Library.

Friends' Library. *See* Monthly Meeting of Friends of New York.

* **Gaelic Society,** 17 West 28th Street, New York City.

"An organization of Irishmen devoted to the study of Irish music history, literature, etc."

Genealogical and Biographical Society. *See* New York Genealogical and Biographical Society.

Genealogical Society. *See* New York Biographical and Genealogical Society.

General Society of Mechanics and Tradesmen of the City of New York, Free Library of the, 16–24 West 44th Street, New York City. Henry W. Parker, Librarian. 94

HISTORY.—Founded 1820, with a nucleus of less than 400 vols.; free public library; supported from public moneys and appropriations from the general funds of the Society. "Historical Sketch" issued in 1900; notice in "Public Libraries in the U. S. A." (Wash., 1876), p. 936–938.

REGULATIONS.—Open 8 A. M.–8 P. M. except Sundays and holidays; reference and circulating; privileges secured upon application.

RESOURCES.—108,728 vols.

General Theological Seminary of the Protestant Episcopal Church, Chelsea Square, Ninth Avenue, between 20th and 21st Streets, New York City. Edward Hurtt Jewett, D.D., Librarian. 95

HISTORY.—Founded 1817; college library; supported by endowment and gifts; income for 1900, $360 from endowment and $1500 from gifts. Historical notices in "Public Libraries in the U. S. A." (Wash., 1876), p. 152–153; Wilson, J. G. "Memorial History of the City of New York" (N. Y., 1893), vol. 4, p. 96–99.

REGULATIONS.—Open 9 A.M.–5 P.M., Saturdays, 9 A.M.–3 P.M.; reference for the public, circulating for members of the Seminary; privileges secured by enrollment as a member of the Seminary.

RESOURCES.—30,023 vols., January 1, 1901; about 20,000 vols. are classified in the *Theological section* and probably 5000 vols. in *Philology* and *History*. This library is the owner of one of the largest—probably the most extensive and complete—collection of *Latin Bibles* in the world. It was collected by W. A. Copinger and was presented to the library by Dean Hoffman. It includes the *Mazarin* or *Gutenberg Bible*, all the *Polyglots*, and a majority of the editions issued before 1500. The section of *Patristics* is very complete, as is also that on the *Councils*.

Geographical Society. *See* American Geographical Society.

George Bruce Branch, New York Public Library. *See* New York Public Library; Astor, Lenox, and Tilden Foundations.

German Hospital and Dispensary in the City of New York, 137 Second Avenue, New York City. Hermann G. Klotz, M.D., Librarian. 96

HISTORY.—Founded 1857; club library; owned by physicians attending the above-named institutions; dues were discontinued in 1898, since which the library has been supported by donations only.

REGULATIONS.—Open 2 P.M.–5 P.M.; reference and circulating; members of the medical profession are admitted on a written introduction from one of the physicians of the German Hospital or Dispensary.

RESOURCES.—5600 vols.; the library principally consists of *Medical Periodicals* in English, German, and French from 1857–1898.

German Liederkranz Library, 111–119 East 58th Street, New York City. G. Otto Wolkwitz, Librarian. 97

History.—Founded December 1, 1868; club library; supported by dues; income for 1900, $1050.

Regulations.—Open Tuesdays and Fridays from 8–11 P.M.; reference and circulating; privileges restricted to membership in the German Liederkranz.

Resources.—7123 vols.; the circulating portion contains only books in the German language.

Girls' High School Library, Nostrand Avenue, Brooklyn, N. Y. Miss M. Josephine Brink, Librarian. 98

History.—Founded 1894; school library; supported from public moneys.

Regulations.—Open 8.30 A.M.–3.00 P.M.; reference library; privileges limited to members of the School.

Resources.—3728 vols. and 50 pamphlets.

Girls' High School Library, Wadleigh High School, 36 East 12th Street, New York City. John G. Wight, Principal. 99

History.—Founded 18--; school library; supported by public moneys.

Regulations.—Open 9 A.M.–2 P.M., during school hours; reference and circulating; privileges enjoyed only by teachers and pupils of the School, and by school officers.

Resources.—910 vols.

Girls' Library. *See* House of Refuge, Randall's Island.

Governor's Island Library. *See* Military Service Institute Library.

Grace House Circulating Library, 802 Broadway, Grace House, New York City. Miss Ella M. Partridge, Librarian. 100

History.—Founded 1881 (formerly the Junior Century Club); free public library; supported by a small endowment.

REGULATIONS.—Open 10 A. M.–10 P. M.; privileges secured by applying to the librarian.

RESOURCES.—About 1700 vols. and 30 pamphlets.

Grammar School No. 99. *See* Public School No. 99.

Grand Lodge F. and A. M. of the State of New York, Masonic Hall, 79 West 23d Street, cor. Sixth Avenue, New York City. Alexander A. Clark, Grand Librarian. 101

HISTORY.—Founded 1868; supported by the Grand Lodge; fraternity library; income for 1900, $1000; no historical notice except report of its librarian in Proceedings.

REGULATIONS.—Open 7–10.30 evenings, except Sundays, and 1.30–5.30 Saturday afternoons; reference only; privileges are extended to any member of the fraternity without any conditions or charges.

RESOURCES.—5000 vols. and a few hundred pamphlets which are quickly bound; the collection is composed of rare *Masonic Works* and *Proceedings of various Grand Lodges.*

Grolier Club, 29 East 32d Street, New York City. Richard Hoe Lawrence, Librarian, H. W. Kent, Assistant Librarian. 102

HISTORY —Founded 1884; club library; supported by dues of Club.

REGULATIONS.—Open 10 A.M.–10 P.M.; reference only; privileges secured by introduction of a member of the Club or by the presentation of the reader's name and address, subject to the regulations of the Club.

RESOURCES.— 7158 vols.; the library is devoted entirely to books on the *Book Arts, Bibliography, Typography, Palæography, Book-binding, Book-illustration,* and *Ex Libris.* The library is unusually rich in *Sale* and *Library Catalogues* and in books on *Printing* and *Incunabula.* It is the desire of the Club that its library be made available, as a library of reference, to all who desire to investigate any of the subjects of which it makes a specialty.

Hahnemannian Library of the New York Medical College. *See* NewYork Homœopathic Medical College and Hospital, Hahnemannian Library.

* **Hall's (Miss) School for Girls Library,** Brooklyn, N. Y. 103

HISTORY.—School library; supported by the School.

REGULATIONS.—Reference and circulating; free to a limited class.

RESOURCES.—About 1800 vols.

Harlem Branch, New York Public Library. *See* New York Public Library; Astor, Lenox, and Tilden Foundations, *also* Young Men's Christian Association, Harlem Branch.

* **Harlem Law Library,** 109 West 125th Street, New York City. W. E. Benjamin, Librarian. 104

HISTORY.—Founded 1891.

RESOURCES.—2500 vols.

Harlem Library, 32 West 123d Street, New York City. Miss Caroline Gaines Thorne, Librarian. 105

HISTORY.—Founded 1825; free to public; supported by public moneys; income for 1900, $7200.

REGULATIONS.—Open 9 A. M.–9 P. M., except Sundays and holidays; reference and circulating; privileges obtained on application with satisfactory reference.

RESOURCES.—14,109 vols.

Harlem Young Women's Christian Association Library, 72–76 West 124th Street, New York City. Mrs. Henry W. Jessup, Chairman of Library Committee. 106

HISTORY.—Founded about 1892; association library; supported by subscription; income for 1900, $50.

REGULATIONS.—Open different hours on different days as classes meet; reference and circulating; privileges secured by becoming a member of the Association.

RESOURCES.—About 1000 vols.; most of the leading magazines may be found in the Reading-room.

Harmonie Club Library, 43 and 45 West 42d Street, New York City. H. Hoffmann, Librarian ; David Lehman, Chairman of the Library Committee. 107

HISTORY.—Founded 1852; supported by an appropriation of the Club; income for 1900, $1700. Historical notice in last catalogue, issued April, 1899.

REGULATIONS.—Open every evening at 8; reference library open day and evening; reference and circulating; for the use of members of the Club and their families only.

RESOURCES.—16,022 vols. and about 400 pamphlets.

Harnett Free Library. *See* St. John's College, Brooklyn.

Harvard Club of New York, 27 West 44th Street, New York City. James Herbert Morse, Jr., Librarian. 108

HISTORY.—Founded 1875; supported from the resources of the Club.

REGULATIONS.—Reference only; privileges of the library are only extended to members.

RESOURCES.—About 5000 volumes; the library consists almost entirely of books and pamphlets written *by Harvard graduates* or *about Harvard University.*

Health Department of the City of New York, 969 Sixth Avenue, New York City. Roger S. Tracy, M.D., Registrar of Records. 109

HISTORY.—Founded 1866; supported by public moneys; additions purchased from contingent fund.

REGULATIONS.—Open 9 A. M.–4 P. M.; reference; used by members of the Department; others can obtain privileges on application to one of the Health Commissioners; exchanges its reports with other similar bodies.

RESOURCES.—1600 vols. and uncounted pamphlets; chiefly statistical, especially Reports upon *Vital Statistics* from all parts of the world.

Hebrew Educational Society of Brooklyn, Pitkin Avenue and Watkins Street, Brooklyn, N. Y. Miss Minnie Shomer, Librarian. 110

Hebrew Educational Society (*continued*).

HISTORY.—Opened September, 1900; free public library; supported by dues from members and public moneys.

REGULATIONS.—Open 10 A. M.–9 P. M., Saturdays from 6–9 P. M.; reference and circulating; privileges secured by placing with librarian a guarantee signed by some responsible person; interchanges books with other libraries.

RESOURCES.—3452 vols. and 172 pamphlets.

Hebrew Institute Library. *See* Aguilar Free Library, 197 East Broadway.

* **Hebrew Orphan Asylum Library,** New York City. D. Adler, Superintendent. 111

HISTORY.—Founded 1876; asylum library; supported by Asylum.

REGULATIONS.—Reference and circulating; free to a limited class.

RESOURCES.—3200 vols.

* **Hebrew Progressive Association Library,** 51 Manhattan Avenue, Brooklyn, N. Y.

Hebrew Technical Institute, 36 Stuyvesant Street, New York City. Edgar S. Burney, Principal. 112

HISTORY.—Established 1887; school library; supported by donations; income for 1900, $228.

REGULATIONS.—Open 12 M.–1 P. M. on school days; reference and circulating; privileges granted to any student of the Institute on application.

RESOURCES.—2437 vols.; devoted especially to works on the Mechanic Trades, *e. g.*, *Woodwork*, *Drawing*, *Electricity*, and *Engineering*.

* **High School Library, Corona,** Corona, N. Y. J. D. Dillingham, in charge. 113

HISTORY.—School library.

RESOURCES.—1188 vols.

High School Library, Flushing, High School Building, Sanford Avenue, Flushing, L. I., N. Y. Jean Ely, Librarian. 114

HISTORY.—Founded 1848; supported by taxation.

REGULATIONS.—Open 8.30 A.M.–8.30 P.M.; reference and circulating; free to pupils of the School only.

RESOURCES.—3454 vols.; places small libraries in the classrooms of the Grammar School.

High School Library, Richmond Hill, High School Building, Elm Street, Richmond Hill, S. I., N. Y. I. N. Failor, Principal. 115

HISTORY.—Founded 1899; supported by public moneys.

REGULATIONS.—Open 9 A.M.–3 P.M.; circulating and reference; free to a limited class.

RESOURCES.—About 1200 vols.

High School Library, Stapleton, Stapleton, S. I., N. Y. A. Hall Burdick, Principal. 116

HISTORY.—Founded 1896; supported by public moneys.

REGULATIONS.—Open 8.30 A.M.–3 P.M.; reference and circulating; free to all pupils and teachers in the School.

RESOURCES.—804 vols.

* **High School Library, Tottenville,** Tottenville, S. I., N. Y. N. J. Lowe, in charge. 117

HISTORY.—Free library.

REGULATIONS.—Open 40 days in the year; 1 hour weekly for circulation.

RESOURCES.—1050 vols.

High School Library. *See also* Public High School Library.

Historical Society, Long Island. *See* Long Island Historical Society.

Historical Society, New York. *See* New York Historical Society.

Holland Society of New York, 348 Broadway, Room 801, New York City. Theodore M. Banta, Secretary. 118

HISTORY.—Founded April 30, 1885; the year books of the Society contain historical matter relating to the library.

REGULATIONS.—Open 9 A.M.–4 P.M.; reference library; privileges of library granted to members of the Society only.

RESOURCES.—About 1000 vols. and 500 pamphlets; this library has in its possession about all of the early *Dutch Church Records* (of New York City ?) that are known to exist. About 600 Dutch books, including the Grotius Collection and many historical works, have been transferred to Columbia University.

Hollis Branch, Queens Borough Library. *See* Queens Borough Library.

HISTORY.—Formerly an independent library, founded in 1897; it was received into the Queens Borough Library, January 1, 1901.

* **Hollis Public School Library,** Hollis, L. I., N. Y. Edna A. Nagle, in charge. 119

HISTORY.—Founded 1897; free to public; income for 1900, $314.67.

REGULATIONS.—Open 208 days in the year; 4 hours each week for circulation.

RESOURCES.—1144 vols.

* **Holy Cross Academy of Manhattan,** 343 West 42d Street, New York City. Mary O'Sullivan, in charge. 120

HISTORY.—Founded 1858; school library; supported by the Academy; income for 1900, $10.

REGULATIONS.—Open 300 days in the year; 12 hours a week for reference and 10 hours for circulation; free to a limited class.

RESOURCES.—1874 vols. and 150 pamphlets.

Homœopathic Medical College, New York. *See* New York Homœopathic Medical College.

Homœopathic Medical Society of the County of New York.

Reports as follows:—"Has no library. The librarian cares for a plaster bust."

* **House of Detention for Witnesses,** 203 Mulberry Street, New York City. James Donovan, in charge. 121

HISTORY.—Founded 1875.
REGULATIONS.—Open daily, 105 hours each week for reference.
RESOURCES.—600 vols.

House of Refuge, Randall's Island, Randall's Island, New York City. Fred C. Helbing, Librarian. 122

HISTORY.—Founded 1825; reform library; supported by endowment.
REGULATIONS.—Reference and circulating; privileges enjoyed only by officers, teachers, and inmates of the Institution.
RESOURCES.—About 3800 vols.; divided into three libraries: Boys' Library; Girls' Library; and Officers' and Teachers' Library.

* **Huger Boarding and Day School Library,** 726 Fifth Avenue, New York City. M. D. Huger, Librarian. 123

HISTORY.—School library; supported by the School.
REGULATIONS.—Reference and circulating; free to a limited class.
RESOURCES.—1200 vols.

Huguenot Society of America, 105 East 22d Street, New York City. Mrs. James M. Lawton, Secretary. 124

HISTORY.—Founded April 13, 1883; an incorporated historical library; supported by dues.
REGULATIONS.—Open 10 A.M.–5 P.M., except Sundays and holidays; free to members and to those introduced by a member.
RESOURCES.—Nearly 1000 vols.; the Society publishes Proceedings and Collections from time to time; exchanges only with libraries having books on Huguenot subjects; historical and genealogical.

Huntington Free Library, Westchester Avenue, Westchester, New York City. Mrs. Collis P. Huntington, President; Miss Elizabeth F. Nisbet, Librarian. 125

HISTORY.—Founded 1891; free to public; supported by endowment.
REGULATIONS.—Hours, 9 A.M.–10 P.M., Sundays, 2–9 P.M.; reference library; every well-behaved person over 14 years of age can gain privileges.
RESOURCES.—6000 vols. and about 30 pamphlets.

Institution for Improved Instruction of Deaf-Mutes, 904 Lexington Avenue, New York City. E. A. Gruver, Principal. 126

HISTORY.—Founded 1867; school library; supported by the Institution.

REGULATIONS.—Open during school hours; reference; privileges obtained by connection with the Institution.

RESOURCES.—1000 vols. and 500 pamphlets; consists of *Deaf-Mute Literature* and works on the *Education of the Deaf*.

Institution for the Blind. *See* New York Institution for the Blind.

Institution for the Instruction of the Deaf and Dumb. *See* New York Institution for the Instruction of the Deaf and Dumb.

Italian Free Reading-Room and Library, 149 Mulberry Street, New York City. Garry Arrighi, Secretary. 127

HISTORY.—Founded July 1, 1894; free public library; supported by endowment of Mrs. A. P. Stokes.

REGULATIONS.—Open 10 A. M.–10 P. M., and on Sundays from 11 A. M.–4 P. M.; free for reference; for circulating, monthly dues of 25 cents are charged.

RESOURCES.—3230 vols.; all books, except about 300, are in the *Italian* language; newspapers are received from the leading Italian cities.

Jackson Square Branch, New York Public Library. *See* New York Public Library; Astor, Lenox, and Tilden Foundations.

Jamaica High School Library, High School Building, Jamaica, L. I., N. Y. Miss Carrie E. Hoyt, Librarian. 128

HISTORY.—Free to public; supported from public moneys; income for 1900, $300.

REGULATIONS.—Open every school-day from 9 A. M.–4 P. M.; circulating; privileges granted on application.

RESOURCES.—About 2100 vols. and 300 pamphlets.

James Black Temperance Library, 3 and 5 West 18th Street, New York City. Rev. Hervey Wood, Librarian. 129

HISTORY.—Founded 1893; society library; this library, representing the life-long collections of the collector, was donated to the National Temperance Society by Mr. James Black, of Lancaster, Pa., at the time of his death in 1893.

REGULATIONS.—Open 9 A. M.–5 P. M.; reference only; privileges secured by application at the office of the Society.

RESOURCES.—1303 vols., about 10,000 pamphlets, and many thousand newspapers; devoted entirely to *Temperance Literature and Statistics* in all its phases. Some of the volumes date back to the seventeenth century and have been gathered from all parts of the world.

Jewish Historical Society. *See* American Jewish Historical Society.

* **Jewish Theological Seminary Library (Morais Library),** 736 Lexington Avenue, New York City. Phineas Israeli, Librarian. 130

HISTORY.—Founded 1886; theological library; supported by Seminary.

REGULATIONS.—Reference library; free to a limited class.

RESOURCES.—About 5000 vols. and 1245 pamphlets.

Junior Century Club. *See* Grace House Circulating Library.

Juvenile Asylum, New York. *See* New York Juvenile Asylum.

* **King's Daughters Settlement,** 48 Henry Street, New York City. Miss Lucy Humphreys, Librarian. 131

REGULATIONS.—Open 1–5 P. M., except Sundays; and on Mondays and Thursdays, 7–9 P. M.

Kingsbridge Library Association, Riverdale Avenue, near Ackerman Street, Kingsbridge, N. Y. Miss Marjorie H. Winn, Librarian. 132

Kingsbridge Library Association (*continued*).

HISTORY.—Founded June, 1894; free to public; the library is owned and supported by Mr. James Douglas, of Spuyten Duyvil, his object being to furnish reading matter to the people of the village.

REGULATIONS.—Open 3–6 and 7–9.30 P.M. daily; reference and circulating; no references required; applicants for privileges must sign the register; children must present a note of permission from parents.

RESOURCES.—1667 vols.

La Salle Academy, 44 Second Street, New York City. Brother E. Edmond, Librarian. 133

HISTORY.—Founded 1848; school library; supported from private school funds.

REGULATIONS.—Open during school hours, 8.30 A.M.–4 P.M.; reference and circulating; privileges enjoyed by students of School.

RESOURCES.—4320 vols.; general library for use of the students and professors.

Law Department Library. *See* Corporation Counsel Library.

Law Institute. *See* New York Law Institute.

Law Library of Brooklyn, County Court House, Brooklyn, N. Y. Alfred J. Hook, Librarian. 134

HISTORY.—Founded January 9, 1850; subscription library; supported by public moneys and dues; income for 1900, $7871.22.

REGULATIONS.—Open 8.45 A.M.–11 P.M., except Sundays and holidays; between June 15 and October 1, the library closes at 5.30 P.M.; reference only; privileges may be obtained by becoming a member.

RESOURCES.—23,699 vols.

Law Library of the Equitable Life Assurance Society. *See* Equitable Life Assurance Society, Law Library.

Law School Library. *See* New York Law School Library.

Lawyers' Club. *See* Equitable Life Assurance Society, Law Library.

League for Social Service Library, 105 East 22d Street, New York City. Mrs. Mary R. Cranston, Librarian. 135

HISTORY.—Founded August, 1898; subscription library; supported by annual dues of $2.00. Josiah Strong, LL.D., President; Dr. William H. Tolman, Secretary.

REGULATIONS.—Open 9 A.M.–5 P.M.; reference only; privileges extended only to members; does not interchange with other libraries.

RESOURCES.—1500 vols. and about 5000 pamphlets on *Sociology*. Particularly strong in works on *Religious* and *Industrial Betterment, Municipal Government, Social Settlement Work,* and allied subjects.

Lenox Library. *See* New York Public Library; Astor, Lenox, and Tilden Foundations.

Liederkranz, German. *See* German Liederkranz Library.

Literarische Gesellschaft von Morrisania, 170th Street, cor. of Third Avenue, New York City. Paul A. Junker, Librarian. 136

HISTORY.—Founded 1883; society library; one-fourth of the annual income of the Society is devoted to the acquisition of works relating to the History of Germans in America and works by German-American authors; income for 1900, $150.

REGULATIONS.—Open 8–9 P.M., the first and third Thursdays of each month; reference and circulating; privileges obtained by joining the Society; dues, $9.00 a year.

RESOURCES.—1800 vols.; the general library consists chiefly of books in the German Language. The special department of *German-American Literature,* referred to above, was started January 1, 1900, and now contains about 60 vols.

Loan Libraries for Ships. *See* American Seamen's Friend Society.

Long Island Historical Society, Pierrepont Street, cor. of Clinton Street, Brooklyn, N. Y. Miss Emma Toedteberg, Librarian. 137

Long Island Historical Society (*continued*).

HISTORY.—Founded 1863; incorporated library; supported by endowments ($129,150) and dues ($2000); income for 1900, $8531.47. Historical notice in "Public Libraries in U. S. A." (1876), p. 353–354; and in "Brooklyn Eagle's History of the City of Brooklyn," vol. 2, p. 773–774. Has special funds for the purchase of: 1. American Biography; 2. Works on Greece, Egypt, and the Holy Land; and 3. Industrial Arts.

REGULATIONS.—Open 8.30 A. M.–9.30 P. M.; reference only; privileges accorded to members of the Society; dues $5.00 a year.

RESOURCES.—64,501 vols.; one of its special collections is that of *American Local History* and *Family Genealogies*. The separate *Family Histories* alone number 2390 vols.

Long Island Railroad Branch, Young Men's Christian Association, 45 Borden Avenue, Long Island City, N. Y. Neason Jones, Secretary. 138

HISTORY.—Founded 1894; institutional library; supported by donations, dues, and appropriations for new books.

REGULATIONS.—Open 9 A. M.–9 P. M.; reference and circulating; privileges enjoyed by members of the Association only.

RESOURCES.—600 vols. and 25 pamphlets.

Lotus Club Library, 556–558 Fifth Avenue, New York City. Chester F. Lord, Secretary. 139

HISTORY.—Founded 1870; club library; supported by dues.

REGULATIONS.—Open from 7 A. M. until the following 1 A. M.; reference library; free to members of Club.

RESOURCES.—2000 vols.

Loyal Legion Temperance Society Library, 112 University Place, New York City.

Maimonides Free Library of District No. 1, I. O. B. B., 723 Lexington Avenue, North-East Corner of 58th Street, New York City. Miss Sara X. Schottenfels, Librarian. 140

HISTORY.—Founded 1852; free public library; supported partly by public moneys and partly by dues; income for 1900, $11,000.

REGULATIONS.—Open 9 A.M.–5 P.M. on Fridays and Sundays; 7–10 P.M., Saturdays; and 9 A.M.–9 P.M. on the remaining days of the week; reference and circulating; privileges secured by furnishing satisfactory reference.

RESOURCES.—65,121 vols.

Manhattan College Library, Broadway and West 131st Street, New York City. Brother Paphylinus, Librarian. 141

HISTORY.—Founded 1853; college library; supported by dues of $2 a year.

REGULATIONS.—Open 3–7.30 P.M. daily; reference library; free to a limited class.

RESOURCES.—10,542 vols. and 1645 pamphlets.

Manhattan State Hospital, East, Main Building, Ward's Island, New York City. Alexander E. Macdonald, Superintendent. 142

HISTORY.—Supported entirely by the State.

REGULATIONS.—Privileges enjoyed exclusively by patients and employés of the Hospital.

RESOURCES.—1815 vols. and 85 pamphlets.

Manual Training High School, 76 Court Street, Brooklyn, N. Y. Miss Mary A. Hall, teacher in charge. 143

HISTORY.—Founded 1895; school library; supported by public moneys.

REGULATIONS.—Open for circulation Wednesdays and Thursdays, 2.30–4 P.M., for reference, 9 A.M.–4 P.M. on school-days; privileges limited to members of the School.

RESOURCES.—3009 vols. and 70 pamphlets.

Maritime Exchange. *See* New York Maritime Exchange.

Masonic Library. *See* Grand Lodge F. and A. M. of the State of New York.

Mechanical Engineers' Library Association, 12 West 31st Street, New York City. Miss Isabel Thornton, Librarian. 144

HISTORY.—Founded 1889; free public library; supported by dues; income from all sources for 1900, $5348.68.

REGULATIONS.—Open 10 A. M.-10 P. M. except Sundays; reference library; privileges free to public.

RESOURCES.—About 6000 vols. and 3000 pamphlets; devoted to *Mechanics* and allied sciences.

Mechanics and Tradesmen, General Society of. *See* General Society of Mechanics and Tradesmen of the City of New York.

Mechanics' Institute Library. *See* General Society of Mechanics and Tradesmen of the City of New York.

* **Medical College and Hospital for Women, Library of the,** 213 West 54th Street, New York City. 145

REGULATIONS.—Free to a limited class.

RESOURCES.—750 vols.

Medical Journal Association.

HISTORY.—For historical notice see "Public Libraries in the U. S. A." (Wash., 1876), p. 944.

Medical Society of the County of Kings, 1313 Bedford Avenue, Brooklyn, N. Y. Albert T. Huntington, Librarian; James M. Winfield, M. D., Directing Librarian. 146

HISTORY. — Founded 1845; free society library; supported by endowment and dues; has a fund of $2000 for the purchase of books; for historical notices see file of "Brooklyn Medical Journal."

REGULATIONS.—Open 10 A. M.-10 P. M.; reference and circulating; the library is free to the general public for purposes of reference; books are circulated to members of the Society only; physicians and surgeons only are eligible to membership; interchanges books with other libraries.

RESOURCES.—About 27,000 vols. and 15,000 pamphlets; entirely a *Medical* library.

Medicine, New York Academy of. *See* New York Academy of Medicine.

Medico-Legal Society Library, 39 Broadway, New York City. Fred. L. Hoffman, Jr., officer in charge. 147

HISTORY.—Founded 1875; society library; supported by donations wholly.

REGULATIONS.—Reference library; privileges secured by meeting with the Society or one of its sections, at $1.50 per annum.

RESOURCES.—1500 vols. and about 2000 pamphlets; *Law, Forensic Medicine,* and some *Medical* works. The books are not now accessible, being in storage.

Mercantile Library Association of New York, Clinton Hall, 13 Astor Place, New York City. William Thaddeus Peoples, Librarian. 148

HISTORY.—Founded 1820; subscription library; supported by dues; income for 1900, $25,564.19. Historical notices in Edwards, Edw., "Memoirs of Libraries" (Lond., 1859), vol. 2, p. 198–200; "Public Libraries in the U. S. A." (Wash., 1876), p. 928–931; Wilson, J. G., "Memorial History of the City of New York" (N. Y., 1893), vol. 4, p. 99–102.

REGULATIONS.—Open 8.30 A. M.–6 P. M.; reference and circulating; privileges secured by becoming a member and paying annual dues; for clerks, $1 initiation fee and $4 a year, for merchants and others, $5 a year. Has a Branch at the Equitable Life Assurance Society's building, 120 Broadway.

RESOURCES.—263,217 vols.; contains the *Tomlinson Collection of Manuscripts Relating to New York During the American Revolution.*

Methodist Historical Society Library. *See* Methodist Library.

Methodist Library, 150 Fifth Avenue, New York City. Rev. John Conable Thomas, M. A., Librarian. 149

HISTORY.—Editors' Library was founded about 50 years ago; Missionary Society Library probably earlier; Methodist Historical Society not over 10 years ago; Methodist Historical Society is supported by dues; Editors' Library, by Methodist Book Concern; and Missionary Society Library, by Missionary Society of the Methodist Episcopal Church.

Methodist Library (*continued*).

REGULATIONS.—Open 8. A.M.–5.30 P.M., Sundays and holidays excepted; reference only; privileges may be obtained by consent of the librarian.

RESOURCES.—About 10,000 vols. and 4000 pamphlets; specialties are *Methodist* and *Missionary Books* and pamphlets (including *Annual Reports, Annual Minutes, etc.*), tracts, and periodicals.

* **Metropolitan Club Library,** Fifth Avenue and 60th Street, New York City. Charles Holt, Librarian. 150

HISTORY.—Founded 1894; society library; supported by Club; income for 1900, $100.

REGULATIONS.—Reference and circulating; free to members.

RESOURCES.—About 2000 vols.

Metropolitan Museum of Art, Central Park, near 82d Street and Fifth Avenue, New York City. William L. Andrews, Honorary Librarian. 151

HISTORY.—Founded 1880; supported by endowment and funds supplied by the Museum; income for 1900, $1015.

REGULATIONS.—Open 10 A.M.–4 P.M.; reference only; privileges of the library may be obtained by applying to the Director of the Museum or to the assistant librarian.

RESOURCES.—6026 vols. and 646 pamphlets; the library is composed chiefly of works on *Art* and *Archæology*.

* **Military Service Institute Library,** Governor's Island, New York City. 152

HISTORY.—Founded 1879; garrison library; supported by the Institute.

REGULATIONS.—Reference and circulating; free to members.

RESOURCES.—About 10,000 vols. and 1000 pamphlets.

Missionary Society for Seamen. *See* Protestant Episcopal Church Missionary Society for Seamen.

Missionary Society Library. *See* Methodist Library.

Mixed High School Library. *See* Boys and Girls' High School Library. 153

Monthly Meeting of Friends of New York, 226 East 16th Street, New York City. John Cox, Jr., Librarian. 154

HISTORY.—Founded 1880; society library; supported by appropriations from the Monthly Meeting.

REGULATIONS.—No specified hours for being open; reference and circulating; privileges secured on application to the librarian.

RESOURCES.—About 500 vols.; this is a library of *books by Friends or about Friends*. There is also on the premises a collection of the early records of Friends' meetings in New York and vicinity which may be examined under the care of the custodian, but not removed.

Morais Library. *See* Jewish Theological Seminary Library.

Morrisania, Literarische Gesellschaft von. *See* Literarische Gesellschaft von Morrisania.

* **Mott Memorial Free Library,** 64 Madison Avenue, New York City. 155

HISTORY.—Chartered 1866; free library.

REGULATIONS.—Open 10 A. M.–5 P. M.; reference only; free to all medical students and physicians, and to the general public.

RESOURCES.—Over 3000 vols.; exclusively on *Medicine* and *Surgery*.

Mount St. Ursula Academy Library, Bedford Park, New York City. Mother M. Fidelis, Librarian. 156

HISTORY.—Founded 1855; school library; supported from general funds.

REGULATIONS.—Open at any time; reference and circulating; privileges secured by entering the Academy as a pupil.

RESOURCES.—1881 vols.

Mount St. Vincent, Academy of. *See* Academy of Mount St. Vincent Library.

Muhlenberg Branch, New York Public Library. *See* New York Public Library; Astor, Lenox, and Tilden Foundations.

Music Libraries. *See*, for REFERENCE: New York Public Library; Astor, Lenox, and Tilden Foundations. For CIRCULATING: Arthur W. Tams Music Library *and* Schirmer (G.) Circulating Library of Music.

National Temperance Society's Library. *See* James Black Temperance Library.

Natural History, American Museum of. *See* American Museum of Natural History.

Navy Yard Library. *See* United States Purchasing and Distributing Library.

Neighborhood Guild Library. *See* University Settlement Library.

Nelson Branch, Queens Borough Library. *See* Queens Borough Library.

New Brighton Free Circulating Library. *See* Free Circulating Library.

New Church, Society of the. *See* Free Library and Reading-Room of the Brooklyn Society of the New Church.

New Utrecht Branch, Brooklyn Public Library. *See* Brooklyn Public Library.

HISTORY.—Formerly an independent library, founded in 1895, it was received into the Brooklyn Public Library, January 1, 1901.

New York Academy of Medicine, 17 West 43d Street, near Fifth Avenue, New York City. John S. Brownne, Resident Librarian. 157

HISTORY.—Organized 1847; incorporated 1851; society library; supported by endowments and dues. There are 12 Library funds with a total amount of $56,502.25 distributed as follows: General Fund, $20,727.55; Anna Woerishoffer Fund, $15,000; Horace Putnam Farnham Fund, $10,000; Phillipine Meyer and Ernest Jacoby Fund, $5035;

Ernst Krackowizer Fund, $1670; James S. Cushman, Dr. Orville Ranney Flower, and William T. Lusk Funds, each $1000; Semi-Centennial Fund, $500; A. L. Northrop Dental Library Fund, $250; Merrill Whitney Williams Fund, $220; and J. Marion Sims Memorial Fund, $100; income for 1900, from above funds, $2128.13; other sources unreported. Historical notice: "Public Libraries in the U.S.A." (Wash., 1876), p. 941–942.

REGULATIONS.—Open 10 A.M.–10 P.M., except Sundays and holidays; reference and circulating to Fellows of the Academy and free to public for reference purposes; interchanges books with other libraries.

RESOURCES.—About 89,000 vols., including 36,105 vols. of duplicates, and 20,000 pamphlets; entirely devoted to *Medical Literature*; has 991 current *Medical Periodicals*, in many languages on file, also many *Reports* and *Transactions of Medical Societies*. The Academy's own publications comprise eleven volumes of Transactions, four volumes of the Bulletin, and some fifty miscellaneous Addresses, Memoirs, Reports, etc. All of these publications are for sale, or will be exchanged for works not already in the library. In March, 1898, the New York Hospital Library of 7000 vols., or, including duplicates, about 23,000 vols., was transferred to the Academy. The Hospital Library, founded in 1796, and located at 6 West 16th Street, was for many years the largest and best equipped Medical Library in the City. A Historical notice of it is contained in "Public Libraries in the U. S. A." (Wash., 1876), p. 923–924.

New York Academy of Sciences, temporarily stored at Room No. 507 Schermerhorn Hall, Columbia University, New York City. Livingston Farrand, Librarian. 158

HISTORY.—Founded 1818.

REGULATIONS.—Open on application to the librarian (better write); reference only; privileges obtained by membership in the Academy.

RESOURCES.—From 8000 to 9000 vols. and from 2000–3000 pamphlets; almost entirely *Scientific*, and is strongest in *Scientific Periodicals* and *Transactions of Learned Societies.*

New York American Veterinary College Library, 141 West 54th Street, New York City. W. J. Coates, M.D., D.V.S., Chairman of Library Committee. 159

New York Amer. Veterinary College Library (*continued*).

HISTORY.—Founded 1875; a department of New York University, formed in 1899 by the union of the New York College of Veterinary Surgeons, chartered in 1857, and the American Veterinary College, chartered in April, 1875; college library; supported by University.

REGULATIONS.—Open during class-hours, 8 A. M.–5 P. M.; privileges enjoyed by students and alumni of the College.

RESOURCES.—1250 vols. and about 1200 pamphlets; devoted to *Medicine and Veterinary Medicine*.

New York Athletic Club Library, Central Park South, corner of 59th Street and Sixth Avenue, New York City. Henry A. S. Upton, Librarian. 160

HISTORY.—Founded 1895; club library; supported by yearly grant of the Club.

REGULATIONS.—Open from 7 A. M. to the following 1 A. M.; reference only; free to those joining the Club.

RESOURCES.—4800 vols. and numerous pamphlets; devoted to general literature and particularly to books in all branches of *Sports*.

New York Botanical Garden Library, Botanical Museum, Bronx Park, New York City. Miss Anna Murray Vail, Librarian. 161

HISTORY.—In addition to the books owned by the New York Botanical Garden, this library contains the botanical library of Columbia University, the botanical portion of the library of the New York Academy of Sciences, and also that of the New York Academy of Medicine. Historical notice in "Journal of the New York Botanical Garden" for February, 1900.

REGULATIONS.—Open 11 A. M.–4 P. M.; reference only; privileges secured by an introduction from the Director-in-Chief.

RESOURCES.—About 10,000 vols. and pamphlets uncounted; especially devoted to *Botany, Horticulture*, and *Landscape Gardening*. The library of the Torrey Botanical Club is deposited here.

New York Caledonian Club Library, 846 Seventh Avenue, New York City. William L. M. Brittain, Secretary. 162

HISTORY.—Founded 1856; club library; supported by Club dues.

REGULATIONS.—Open 8 A. M.–11.30 P. M.; reference and circulating; free to members only; privileges secured by membership in Club (Scotchmen or their descendants, only, being eligible).

RESOURCES.—5000 vols.

New York Catholic Protectory Library, Female Department, West Chester, New York City. Sister M. Antoninus, Librarian. 163

HISTORY.—Founded 1872; school library; supported by donations.

REGULATIONS.—Reference and circulating; free to a limited class.

RESOURCES.—About 1800 vols. and 100 pamphlets.

* **New York Catholic Protectory Library, Male Department.** New York City. Brother William, Librarian. 164

HISTORY.—Founded 1867; school library; supported by the School.

REGULATIONS.—Reference and circulating; free to a limited class.

RESOURCES.—5670 vols. and about 800 pamphlets.

* **New York Chapter of the American Institute of Architects,** 215 West 57th Street, New York City. Charles I. Berg, Secretary.

New York Christian Home for Intemperate Men, formerly at 1175 Madison Avenue, cor. 86th Street, New York City. 165

HISTORY.—Founded about 1878; the library contains a few hundred volumes for the use of the inmates only. The institution is now located at Chester Crest, Mount Vernon, N. Y.

New York City Free Public Libraries.

Alphabetical list with appropriations made by the Board of Estimate and Apportionment in their Budget for the year 1902. For particulars of each library, see under its name in the general list.

AGUILAR FREE LIBRARY	$ 38,000.00
BROOKLYN PUBLIC LIBRARY	150,000.00
CATHEDRAL FREE CIRCULATING LIBRARY	17,275.00

New York City Free Public Libraries (*continued*).

General Society of Mechanics and Tradesmen of the City of New York	$6,150.00
Harlem Library	8,300.00
Maimonides Free Library of District No. 1, I. O. B. B.	10,000.00
New York Free Circulating Library for the Blind	677.70
New York Public Library; Astor, Lenox, and Tilden Foundations	85,650.00
Queens Borough Library	20,000.00
Tenement House Chapter Library	950.00
Tottenville Library Association	1,116.10
University Settlement Library	4,500.00
Washington Heights Free Library	5,500.00
Webster Free Library	6,800.00
Young Men's Benevolent Association Free Circulating Library	4,025.00
Young Women's Christian Association of the City of New York	5,900.00

New York City Hall Library. *See* City Library.

New York City Mission and Tract Society. *See* Broome Street Free Library.

New York City Public School Libraries.

For the names and location of the various schools consult the directories, for 1901, of the Boroughs of Manhattan and the Bronx, Brooklyn, Queens, and Richmond.

History.—The first public school library was founded in Public School No. 1 in 1810 by The Public School Society. In 1818 each school was provided. The several schools subsequently established received libraries as a necessary part of their apparatus. In 1835 measures were adopted to procure libraries for the use of trustees and teachers. By the provisions of Chapter 237 of the Laws of 1838, the city received annually $10,000, its proportion from the United States Deposit Fund, "to be applied either to the support of School Libraries or to the payment of teachers." The money was used for salaries. In 1860 the legislature prohibited the appropriation of this money for any other purpose than the purchase of books for school libraries. Yearly accessions soon gave the schools substantial equipment. About 1880 each school had bequeathed to it $250 worth of books, known as the Holbrook Library. Shortly thereafter the American Museum of Natural History presented each school with a case of natural history specimens and a copy, in four quarto volumes, of Cassell's "Popular Natural History." By the provisions of Chapter 566 of the Laws of 1894, increased state aid was furnished for the purchase of school libraries. The first appropriation served to replace worn reference books and to procure later publications. A subsequent appropriation was used almost entirely for the purchase of books for the scholars.

REGULATIONS.—Open every school-day from 8.30 A. M. to 3.30 P. M.; the general library for reference, the class libraries for circulation and home reading. Lists of suggested reading are posted in the classrooms. Privileges restricted to those directly connected with the schools.

RESOURCES.—600,000 volumes, comprising (1) reference books for use in the schools; (2) books especially designed as aids to teachers; (3) books relating to branches of study pursued in the schools; (4) supplementary reading books, including (a) books that cultivate a taste for good reading in the pupils, and (b) those that give information on the subjects prescribed in the Course of Study. Number of schools, 516. Income, $50,000 annually, half from the City and half from the State.

Detailed information respecting some of these libraries may be found in this list.

New York College of Veterinary Surgeons. *See* New York American Veterinary College Library.

New York Colored Mission Library, 135 West 30th Street, New York City. Mrs. Margaret W. Symmes, Librarian. 166

REGULATIONS.—Open Fridays, 4–5 P. M.

* **New York Eye and Ear Infirmary Library,** 222 Second Avenue, New York City. 167

HISTORY.—Founded 1849; institutional library; supported by the Infirmary.

REGULATIONS.—Reference only; free to a limited class.

RESOURCES.—About 1000 vols. and 3000 pamphlets; largely composed of *Medical* works.

New York Free Circulating Library. *See* New York Public Library; Astor, Lenox, and Tilden Foundations.

New York Free Circulating Library for the Blind, 121 West 91st Street, New York City. Miss Helen M. Ferry, Librarian. 168

HISTORY.—Founded June 3, 1895; free library; supported by subscriptions, donations, and public moneys; income for 1900, $870.30.

REGULATIONS.—Open 1–4 P. M., on Mondays, Wednesdays, Thursdays, and Saturdays; circulating; privileges obtained by furnishing satisfactory reference.

RESOURCES.—1440 vols. and 382 pieces of *Music*.

New York Genealogical and Biographical Society, 226 West 58th Street, New York City. Hiram Calkins, Jr., Secretary and Librarian. 169

HISTORY.—Founded March, 1869; subscription library; supported by endowment and dues. Historical notice in "Public Libraries in the U. S. A." (Wash., 1876), p. 357.

REGULATIONS.—Open 10 A. M.–6 P. M. daily except Sundays; Mondays, 8–10 P. M.; reference only; privileges obtained by membership or introduction by a member.

RESOURCES.—About 5000 vols. and about 6000 pamphlets. Specialty: *Genealogy* and *Local History*.

New York Historical Society, 170 Second Avenue, corner of East 11th Street, New York City. Robert H. Kelby, Librarian. 170

HISTORY.—Founded 1804 and incorporated in 1809; society library; supported by dues of members and endowments; it has a special fund for the purchase of Local Histories and Genealogies. Historical notices: "Public Libraries in the U. S. A." (Wash., 1876), p. 357–358, 924–928; Wilson, J. G., "Memorial History of New York City" (N. Y., 1893), vol. 4, p. 103–105; and New York Historical Society, "Circular to Members," 1885, p. 9–12.

Regulations.—Open 9 A.M.–6 P.M. except Sundays, legal holidays, and the month of August; reference only; privileges obtained by membership in the Society, or by card or letter from members to those not connected with the Society; its publications are exchanged with those of kindred institutions.

Resources.—Over 100,000 vols.; devoted to *American History, Travels* and *Cartography;* it has one of the largest special collections in this country relative to American *Local History* and *Genealogy* and is also particularly strong in *American Newspapers* printed prior to 1800; its archives include many important American historical manuscripts; the Society's Cabinet includes the excellent Abbott Collection of Egyptian antiquities, and also Nineveh sculptures; while among its art objects are about 875 paintings and 65 pieces of sculpture.

New York Homœopathic Medical College and Hospital, Hahnemannian Library, 63d Street and Avenue A, near East 63d Street, New York City. George Jansen, Librarian. 171

History.—Founded 1885; college library; supported by subscriptions.

Regulations.—Open 10 A.M.–5 P.M. except Sundays and holidays; reference library; free to students of the College.

Resources.—About 5000 vols. and 7420 pamphlets; purely a Medical reference library.

New York Hospital Library. *See* New York Academy of Medicine.

New York House of Refuge, Randall's Island. *See* House of Refuge, Randall's Island.

* **New York Institution for the Blind, Library of the,** 412 Ninth Avenue, between 33d and 34th Streets, New York City. William B. Wait, in charge. 172

History.—Founded 1831, incorporated 1837; free school library; supported by the Institution; income for 1900, $573.58.

Regulations.—Open 278 days in the year; 84 hours each week for reference and 2 hours for circulation; free to a limited class.

Resources.—5047 vols.

New York Institution for the Instruction of the Deaf and Dumb, Broadway and West 163d Street, New York City. Thomas Francis Fox, A.M., Librarian. 173

HISTORY.—Founded 1829; school library; supported by endowment; income for 1900, $4278.61. Historical notice in Preface to Catalogue published in 1893.

REGULATIONS.—Open 9 A.M.–4 P.M., and 7–8 P.M., Mondays; reference and circulating; privileges restricted to directors, teachers, officers, and pupils of the School.

RESOURCES.—7984 vols. and 16,740 pamphlets; special collection relating to the *Education of the Deaf, Treatment of Deafness, Science of Speech Teaching for the Deaf, etc.*, about 600 vols.; a special collection of 200 vols. of miscellaneous works, donated by the Hon. Frederick De Peyster, LL.D., forms the "De Peyster Alcove" of the Library.

New York Juvenile Asylum, 176th Street and Amsterdam Avenue, New York City. Charles E. Bruce, M.D., Superintendent. 174

HISTORY.—Founded 1851; supported by appropriation from Maintenance Fund.

RESOURCES.—Teachers' Reference Library, about 400 vols.; Children's Library, about 500 vols.

New York Law Institute, Post Office Building, Rooms 116–122, 4th and 5th Floors, New York City. William H. Winters, Librarian. 175

HISTORY.—Founded 1828, chartered Feb. 22, 1830; supported by dues only; income for 1900, $16,529.61. Historical notices: "The Library of the New York Law Institute," by William H. Winters, in his "History of the Bench and Bar of New York" (New York, 1897), vol. 1, p. 210–225; Report of the Librarian, N. Y., 1899; also "Public Libraries in the U. S. A." (Wash., 1876), p. 938.

REGULATIONS.—Open 9 A.M.–10 P.M. except Sundays; reference and circulating; privileges only secured by election to membership by vote of the Executive Committee; initiation fee, $35; annual dues, $20; life membership, $75; interchanges books with other libraries.

RESOURCES.—54,399 vols. and 728 pamphlets; the library consists entirely of law literature including *Law Reports, Periodicals, Statutes, Codes, etc.*

New York Law School Library, 35 Nassau Street, New York City. Miss Lucy D. Waterman, Librarian. 176

HISTORY.—Founded 1898; educational library; supported by endowment.

REGULATIONS.—Open 9 A.M.–7 P.M.; reference only; free to all students of the School; others must obtain permit from the Dean; have not yet interchanged books with other libraries.

RESOURCES.—7325 vols.; contains the ordinary resources of a working law library—*Reports, Statutes, Text-Books, etc.* Takes 28 sets of continuations.

New York Maritime Exchange Library, occupies part of the Maritime Exchange, 12 Beaver Street, New York City. A. J. Hennessy, Acting Superintendent. 177

HISTORY.—Founded 1874; club library.

REGULATIONS.—Open 8 A.M.–6 P.M.; reference, for members only.

RESOURCES.—About 1600 vols. and about 200 pamphlets; chiefly relating to *Law* and *Maritime matters.*

New York Penitentiary, Blackwell's Island. *See* Blackwell's Island Penitentiary Library.

* **New York Port Society Library,** 46 Catherine Street, New York City. 178

HISTORY.—West Side Branch, 128 Charlton Street.

REGULATIONS.—Open from 9 A.M.–10 P.M.; for use of seamen and congregation of the Mariners' Church.

New York Post Graduate Medical School and Hospital, 20th Street and 2d Avenue, New York City. Alexander H. Candlish, Superintendent. 179

HISTORY.—Founded 1882; educational library; supported from funds of the Institution.

REGULATIONS.—Open 9 A.M.–10.30 P.M.; reference only; privileges secured by matriculating in the School.

RESOURCES.—416 vols.; 236 current *Medical Journals* on file.

New York Press Club, 116 Nassau Street, New York City. Charles Hemstreet, Librarian. 180

HISTORY.—Founded 1872; club library; supported by endowment.

REGULATIONS.—Open all hours, night and day; reference only; privileges secured by club membership.

RESOURCES.—About 6000 vols.; general library.

New York Produce Exchange, Broadway and Beaver Street, New York City. James F. Partrick, Librarian. 181

HISTORY.—Founded 1862; society library.

REGULATIONS.—Open 9 A. M.–4 P. M.; reference only; privileges secured by membership in Exchange and by introduction; Annual reports (a valuable book of statistics) sent to various libraries.

RESOURCES.—3500 pamphlets; library is mainly statistical.

New York Public Library; Astor, Lenox, and Tilden Foundations. Administration Offices, 40 Lafayette Place, New York City. John Shaw Billings, LL.D., Director. 182

Reference Libraries.—1. ASTOR LIBRARY BUILDING, 40 Lafayette Place; offices of the Director and of I. Ferris Lockwood, Business Supt.; Charles H. A. Bjerregaard in charge of Reading Rooms.—2. LENOX LIBRARY BUILDING, 895 Fifth Avenue, between 70th and 71st Streets; Wilberforce Eames, Librarian in charge; Victor H. Paltsits, in charge of Reading Rooms. A new building is in course of construction on Fifth Avenue, between 40th and 42d Streets.

Circulating Branches.—Arthur Elmore Bostwick, Ph.D., Chief of the Circulation Department, 226 West 42d St.—1. BOND STREET BRANCH, 49 Bond Street, established March 15, 1880, Miss Marie C. Saxer in charge.—2. OTTENDORFER BRANCH, 135 Second Avenue, Dec. 8, 1884, Miss Hedwig M. Goeks in charge.—3. GEORGE BRUCE BRANCH, 226 West 42d Street, Jan. 6, 1888, Miss Isabel de Treville in charge.—4. JACKSON SQUARE BRANCH, 251 West 13th Street, July 6, 1888, Miss Elizabeth C. Thayer in charge.—5. HARLEM BRANCH, 218 East 125th Street, July, 1892, Miss Alice Brown in charge.—6. MUHLENBERG BRANCH, 130 West 23d Street, February, 1893, Miss Evelyn R. Andrews in charge.—7. BLOOMINGDALE BRANCH, 206 West 100th Street, June 3, 1896, Miss Eugenie Krauss in charge.—8. RIVERSIDE BRANCH, 230 Amsterdam Avenue, near 70th Street, 1894; received as a branch of the New York Free Circulating Library May 26, 1897, Miss Kate Kaufman in charge.—9. YORKVILLE BRANCH, 1523 Second Avenue, June 10, 1897, Miss Minerva E. Grimm in charge.— 10. THIRTY-FOURTH STREET BRANCH, 215 East 34th Street, June 6, 1898, Miss Lucie B. Bohmert in charge.—11. CHATHAM SQUARE BRANCH, 22 East Broadway, July 5, 1899, Miss Hildegard M. Steinberger in charge.—12. ST. AGNES BRANCH, 2279 Broadway, January, 1894; received as a branch of the New York Public Library, July, 1901, Miss Anne L. Gibson in charge.—13. WASHINGTON HEIGHTS BRANCH, 922 St. Nicholas Avenue, 1868; received as a branch of the New York Public Library, Dec. 1, 1901, Miss Alma R. Van Hoevenberg in charge.—TRAVELLING LIBRARIES, 206 West 100th Street, April, 1897, Miss Adeline E. Brown in charge.

HISTORY.—Organized May 23, 1895, by consolidation of the Astor Library, 260,000 vols., incorporated Jan. 18, 1849; the Lenox Library, 86,000 vols., incorporated Jan. 20, 1870; and the Tilden Trust, 20,000 vols., incorporated March 26, 1887. Reorganized Feb. 25, 1901, by consolidating with the New York Free Circulating Library, 170,000 vols., incorporated March 15, 1880. The Library, as at present constituted (February, 1902), consists of two Reference Libraries, and thirteen Circulating Branches, as stated above.

HISTORICAL NOTICES.—ASTOR LIBRARY: Guild, R. A., "Librarian's Manual," (N. Y., 1858), sketch by Dr. Jos. G. Cogswell, Supt., p. 185–189; Edwards, Edw., " Memoirs of Libraries" (Lond., 1859), vol. 2, p. 218–226; "Public Libraries in the U. S. A." (Wash., 1876), p. 931–936; Wilson, J. G., "Memorial History of City of New York" (N. Y., 1893), vol. 4, p. 78–85, and Saunders, F., in *Woman*, v. 1, p. 17, 73 —LENOX LIBRARY: "Public Libraries in the U. S. A." (1876), p. 946–950; Stevens, Henry, "Recollections of Mr. James Lenox" (Lond., 1886); Wilson, J. G., "Memorial History," vol. 4, p. 88–96.—Library of Hon. Samuel J. TILDEN: "Bulletin of N.Y. Pub. Library," vol. 3, p. 4–8. *See also* "Hand-book of New York Public Library," "Bulletin of N.Y. Pub. Lib., " vol. 1, p. 3–10, "Final Report of N. Y. Free Circulating Library" (N. Y., 1900), pp. 20–25, and entries in "Poole's Index."

REGULATIONS.—Reference Department Astor and Lenox buildings open 9 A.M.–6 P.M. on week-days except New Year's day, July 4th, and Christmas day of each year. Circulating Department, Free Circulating Branches, open 9 A.M.–9 P.M. on every week-day except Christmas, New

New York Public Library (*continued*).

Year's day, July 4th, Thanksgiving day, Decoration day, and Presidential election days. On other election days they close at 5 P. M., and on Washington's Birthday and Christmas eve at 6 P. M. Privileges: Reference reading-rooms at Astor and Lenox buildings, and at such of the Branches as maintain separate reading-space, are free to all respectable persons; a security blank is required to be filled out for privilege of withdrawing books from the Circulating Branches, which is further restricted to residents of New York City more than ten years of age. This library occasionally interchanges books with other libraries for circulation.

RESOURCES.—Reference Libraries, Astor and Lenox buildings, 538,957 vols. and 182,370 pamphlets. Circulating Branches, 212,802 vols. Total, 751,759 vols.

Special Collections. — *American Genealogy* and *Local History*, 12,000 vols., John Jonathan Whittle in charge (Lenox). — *American Newspapers* before 1800, 35,000 numbers (Lenox). — *Americana* and Geographical Literature printed before 1800, 20,000 vols. (Lenox).— *Angling*, Waltoniana, etc., 600 vols. (Lenox).—*Bibles*, including the library of the American Bible Society, deposited in 1897, 8000 vols. (Lenox).—*Bunyan's* "Pilgrim's Progress," etc., 500 vols. (Lenox).— *Don Quixote* Collection, given by Rev. Wendell Prime, 450 vols. (Lenox).—*Dutch History*, 480 vols., 10,000 pm. (Astor).—*Economics, Finance and Banking*, including the Gordon L. Ford Collection, 6700 vols., 3000 pm. (Astor).—*Hebrew* Collection, including purchases from the Jacob H. Schiff Fund for Semitic Literature, 6000 vols., Abraham Solomon Freidus in charge (Astor).—*Incunabula*, or European 15th Century books, Mexican 16th Century books, and Anglo-American 17th Century books, 600 vols. (Lenox).—*Manuscripts*, 75,000 separate pieces, 1000 bound vols., George De C. Curtis in charge (Lenox).—*Maps*, 5000 sheets, 300 atlases, many of very early date (Lenox).— *Mathematics*, 3600 vols. (Astor).— *Music*, 10,000 vols., including the Drexel Collection of 6,000 vols., Miss Rebecca McElhone in charge (Lenox).—*Naval History*, etc., including purchases from the James Owen Proudfit Fund, 660 vols., 300 pm. (Astor).—*Needlework, Embroidery*, etc., 200 vols., 120 pm. (Astor).—*Oriental* Department, excluding Hebrew, but including purchases from the Jacob H. Schiff Fund for Semitic Literature, 3000 vols., Prof. Richard James Horatio Gottheil in charge (Astor).—*Patents*, 10,000 vols. (Astor).—*Periodical* Department, 4000 current serials (Astor).— *Print* Department,

35,000 separate prints, 1000 bound vols. (Lenox).—*Public Documents*, 60,000 vols., Miss Adelaide R. Hasse in charge (Astor).—*Railroad Collection*, 2500 vols., 5100 pm. (Astor). — *Shakespeare Collection*, including the early quarto and folio editions of the Plays, 3000 vols. (Lenox).—*Slavonic Literature*, 2000 vols., Herman Rosenthal in charge (Astor).—*Sociology*, including the collection given by F. A. Sorge, and the collections relating to *Pauperism* and *Criminology* from the Richard L. Dugdale Fund, 2100 vols., 1770 pm. (Astor).—*Sports and Pastimes*, including gifts of John L. Cadwalader, 3000 vols. (Astor).

EXHIBITIONS.—Two Art Galleries at the Lenox containing about 400 Paintings; Show Cases and Screens for Prints, Rare Books, Maps, etc., in the Halls of the Astor and Lenox Buildings.

New York School of Applied Design for Women, 200 West 23d Street, New York City. Miss Mary Whittredge, Librarian. 183

HISTORY.—Founded 1892; educational library; supported by School.

REGULATIONS.—Open 9.30 A.M.–4.30 P.M., Saturdays, 9.30 A.M.–12.30 P.M.; reference only; privileges enjoyed by students of the School.

RESOURCES.—566 vols. and 5280 pamphlets; entirely devoted to works on *Design*.

New York Society Library, 109 University Place, New York City. Frank Barna Bigelow, Librarian. 184

HISTORY.—Founded as "a Public Library" in 1700, reorganized in 1754; subscription library; supported by endowment and dues; income for 1900, $15,733.41. Historical notices: MacMullen, John, "Lecture on the past, the present, and the future of the N. Y. Society Library" (N. Y., 1856); Edwards, Edward, "Memoirs of Libraries" (Lond., 1856), vol. 2, p. 189–191; "Public Libraries in the U. S. A." (Wash., 1876), p. 14–15, 919–923; Wilson, J. G., "Memorial History of New York City" (N. Y., 1893), vol. 4, p. 106–109; "Charters and By-Laws of the Library," (1881), and *Library Journal* (1894), v. 19, p. 231–232.

REGULATIONS.—Open 9 A.M.–6 P.M., reading room, 9 A.M.–9 P.M.; reference and circulating; privileges obtained by membership; transferable right, $25, subject to annual payment of $10; temporary subcription, $10 a year, $6 for six months, $4 for three months; free shares, $150; sometimes interchanges books with other libraries.

New York Society Library (*continued*).

RESOURCES.—About 100,000 vols.; special features are *Early Newspapers, Fine Arts; Americana*, especially New York. This library possesses 100 vols. of the first library established in New York in the year 1700. It also possesses the library of John Winthrop 2d.

New York Society of Pedagogy, Public School Building No. 6, East 85th Street and Madison Avenue, New York City. Miss Emma Hawthorn, Custodian. 185

HISTORY.—Founded 1894; society library; supported by dues of members and State aid.

REGULATIONS.—Open 3–6 P. M., on school-days; Saturdays, 9 A. M.–6 P. M.; reference and circulating; privileges secured by becoming a member of the Society; all teachers eligible to membership; dues, $2 a year.

RESOURCES.—About 1600 vols. and 200 pamphlets, consisting of books relating to *Teaching* and files of the leading *Educational Periodicals;* one of the best Pedagogical libraries in the city.

New York State Medical Association Library, 64 Madison Avenue, New York City. Miss Alice Dunn, Clerk.

New York Trade School, First Avenue, 67th and 68th Streets, New York City. H. V. Brill, General Manager. 186

HISTORY.—Educational library.

REGULATIONS.—For students of the School only.

RESOURCES.—About 600 vols.; technical and general works about equally divided.

New York Turnverein Library, 85th Street, cor. of Lexington Avenue, New York City. Bernard Strauss, Librarian. 187

HISTORY.—Founded 1850; club library.

REGULATIONS.—Open Tuesdays, 8–9 P. M.; Saturdays, 7.30–8.30 P. M.; privileges enjoyed by members of the Turnverein.

RESOURCES.—About 8000 vols. and 3000 pamphlets.

New York Typothetæ. *See* Typothetæ of New York.

New York University, General Library, University Heights, New York City. Leslie J. Tompkins, Chief Librarian; Miss Belle Corwin, M.D., Assistant Librarian. 188

HISTORY.—Founded 1831; supported by endowment.

REGULATIONS.—Open during term-time, 9 A. M.–5 P. M., except Sundays and holidays; on Saturdays, 9 A. M–1 P. M; reference library; interchanges books with other libraries.

RESOURCES.—About 40,000 vols. and 10,000 pamphlets; special collections : *De Lagarde Semitic Library*, 5500 vols., *Ottendorfer Germanic Library*, 9000 vols., *Botta Italian Library*, 2000 vols.

New York University, Law School Library, University Building, 100 Washington Square East, cor. Waverly Place, New York City. Leslie J. Tompkins, Secretary. 189

HISTORY.—First designated as a Law Library in 1866; income for 1900, $3887.27; supported by income of the School.

REGULATIONS.—Open daily, except Sundays, from 9 A. M.–11 P. M., on Saturdays, 9 A. M.–9 P. M., except during June, July, August, and September, when it is open from 9 A. M.–6 P. M.; reference library; privileges obtained only by becoming a member of the School.

RESOURCES.—14,502 vols.; in 1866 John Taylor Johnson gave his law library, consisting of some 5000 volumes, to the University. This gift formed the basis of the present library, which for some time was called the Johnson Law Library.

* **New York University, School of Pedagogy Library,** University Building, 100 Washington Square East, cor. Waverly Place, New York City. Francis M. Woodward, Assistant Librarian. 190

HISTORY.—Founded 1890; supported from moneys of the School; income for 1900, $757.48.

REGULATIONS.—Open 9 A. M.–6 P. M. during term-time; reference and circulating; privileges secured by becoming a member of the School.

RESOURCES.—4920 vols.; The library is made up of works selected because of their bearing directly upon the subject of *Pedagogy*.

New York University, Veterinary Library. *See* New York American Veterinary College Library.

New York Yacht Club Library, 39 to 41 West 44th Street, New York City. Theodore C. Zerega, Chairman of Library Committee. 191

HISTORY.—Founded 1886; club library; supported by dues; income for 1900, $1900.

REGULATIONS.—Open whenever the Club is open; reference privileges obtained by joining the Club.

RESOURCES.—3400 vols.; a *Nautical Library* only; 362 *Charts* in the collection.

Normal College Alumnæ House Library, 446 East 72d Street, New York City. Miss Jessie L. Biegler, Librarian. 192

HISTORY.—Settlement library; supported by donations of books.

REGULATIONS.—Open Mondays and Thursdays from 4–6 P. M. and from 7–9 P. M.; reference and circulating; privileges granted to those who live in the neighborhood, who can sign a slip and get a satisfactory reference.

RESOURCES.—About 1400 vols.; the Aguilar Free Library furnishes this library with a travelling library.

Normal College Library, 69th Street and Park Avenue, New York City. Miss Edith Rice, Librarian. 193

HISTORY.—Founded 1886; supported from moneys appropriated for College expenses.

REGULATIONS.—Open 8.30 A. M.–4 P. M. on school days; reference and circulating; full privileges accorded to any student in the College and to any member of the Associate Alumnæ.

RESOURCES.—6422 vols.; pamphlets about 5000; specialties: *German Classics* in Neustadt Memorial Alcove in charge of Prof. I. Kellar, 372 vols. and 865 paper vols. (for class use); Wadleigh Memorial Alcove, for the use of the College Staff, 310 vols. on *Philosophy, Ethics, etc.*; Covell Memorial Alcove, in charge of Miss M. C. W. Reid, 73 vols. on *Art*; 250 vols. on *Psychology and Education*, in charge of Dr. Emily Ida Conant.

Numismatic and Archæological Society. *See* American Numismatic and Archæological Society.

Officers' and Teachers' Library. *See* House of Refuge, Randall's Island.

Olivet Memorial Church Library, 59 to 63 Second Street, New York City. Miss Anna Cronenbold, Librarian. 194

HISTORY.—Free public library.

REGULATIONS.—Open 9 A. M.–9 P. M., except Sundays and holidays; reference and circulating; privileges secured on furnishing suitable reference.

RESOURCES.—About 3000 vols.

Ottendorfer Branch, New York Public Library. *See* New York Public Library; Astor, Lenox, and Tilden Foundations.

Ozone Park Branch, Queens Borough Library. *See* Queens Borough Library.

HISTORY.—Formerly an independent library, founded in 1897; it was received into the Queens Borough Library, January 1, 1901.

Packer Collegiate Institute Library, 170 Joralemon Street, Brooklyn, N. Y. Miss Julia B. Anthony, Librarian. 195

HISTORY.—Founded in 1845 as the Library of the Brooklyn Female Academy; school library; supported from the general funds of the Institute; expenditures for 1900, $310.

REGULATIONS.—Open 8.45 A. M.–5 P. M. on five days of the week during school terms; open to teachers on Saturdays and during vacations; reference and circulating; free to a limited class.

RESOURCES.—8057 vols. The library has ten subscriptions at the Brooklyn Library and the privilege of drawing extra books, at a cost to the Institute of about $60 a year.

Paulist Parish Library. *See* Columbian Reading Union.

Peck Memorial Library. *See* Public School No. 87.

Pedagogy, School of. *See* New York University, School of Pedagogy.

Penitentiary Library, Blackwell's Island. *See* Blackwell's Island Penitentiary Library.

Peter Cooper High School. *See* Boys' and Girls' High School Library.

Pharmacy, College of. *See* College of Pharmacy of the City of New York.

Physicians to the German Hospital and Dispensary in the City of New York. *See* German Hospital and Dispensary in the City of New York.

* **Players' Club Library,** 16 Gramercy Park, New York City. Edwin B. Child, Librarian. 196

HISTORY.—Founded 1888; club library; supported by the Club.

REGULATIONS.—Reference only; free to members.

RESOURCES.—2123 vols.

Polish Benevolent Society Library, 13 Market Street, New York City.

Polytechnic Institute of Brooklyn, Library of the Academic Department, Livingston Street, near Court, Brooklyn, N. Y. William Warner Bishop, Librarian. 196a

HISTORY.—Founded, 1899; school library; supported by the Corporation and by State funds; income for 1899–1900, $1000.

REGULATIONS.—Open 8.30 A. M.–3.30 P. M. for reference and circulation; privileges extended to students of the School and to properly introduced visitors.

RESOURCES.—2500 volumes.

Polytechnic Institute of Brooklyn. *See also* Spicer Memorial Library.

Poppenhusen Institute Library, College Point, Long Island, N. Y. William Harper, Superintendent. 197

HISTORY.—Founded 1868, and a part of the Conrad Poppenhusen Association's Institute; free to public; supported by endowment; income for 1900, for purchase of books and pamphlets, $250.

REGULATIONS.—Open 7–9 P.M. for circulation; open all day for reference; privileges granted by guaranty of one citizen.

RESOURCES.—3242 vols. and about 220 pamphlets; the library is one of the educational features of the Conrad Poppenhusen Association.

Post Graduate Medical School and Hospital. *See* New York Post Graduate Medical School and Hospital.

Pratt Institute Free Library, 215 Ryerson Street, near De Kalb Avenue, Brooklyn, N. Y. Miss Mary Wright Plummer, Director. 198

HISTORY.—Founded 1888; free to public; supported by endowment; income for 1900, $33,000. Historical notice in "Pratt Institute Monthly," June, 1896, and December, 1900. The Astral Branch, 184 Franklin Street, near Java Street, founded in 1888, 7067 vols., was transferred to the Brooklyn Public Library September 16, 1901.

The Library School connected with this library began in 1890 with a Training Class, chiefly for the purpose of supplying vacancies in the library's own staff. The Class has grown into a School, which offers a general course of one year and two special second-year courses, one for the training of children's librarians and one a historical and bibliographical course. Information in regard to these courses may be had on application to the Director of the Library.

REGULATIONS.—Open, reading and reference rooms, 9 A.M.–9.30 P.M.; circulating department same, except on Tuesdays, Thursdays, and Fridays, when the hours are from 9 A.M.–6 P.M.; reference and circulating; privileges secured by presenting written application and securing a Brooklyn citizen as reference; would probably be willing to interchange books with other libraries in some cases.

RESOURCES.—About 82,046 vols. and 109 bound vols. of pamphlets classified by subjects (Sept. 15, 1901); specialties: 218 *Magazines* indexed by Poole are subscribed for and almost as many sets owned by the library; *Mounted Photograph Collection* numbers 17,000 pieces; *Text-book Collection*, a beginning of about 200 vols.

Press Club Library. *See* New York Press Club.

Produce Exchange. *See* New York Produce Exchange.

Prospect Branch, Brooklyn Public Library. *See* Brooklyn Public Library.

Protestant Episcopal Church Missionary Society for Seamen, East River Station, 34 Pike Street, New York City. Rev. Archibald Romaine Mansfield, Chaplain; Frank Hughes, Librarian. 199

HISTORY.—A free reading-room and game-room for seamen only.

REGULATIONS.—Open daily, including Sundays, 9 A. M.–10 P. M.

"We have in this institution a Reading-Room for Seamen; *it is not a library in any sense of the term,* although it is often advertised as such."

Protestant Episcopal Seaman's Society; Out-door Station. *See* Cummings Library.

* **Public High School Library,** Jamaica, L. I., N. Y. Miss Carrie E. Hoyt, in charge. 200

HISTORY.—Founded 1860; school library; supported by taxation; free to public.

REGULATIONS.—Open 180 days in the year; 38 hours each week for circulation; reference and circulating.

RESOURCES.—About 2000 vols. and 150 pamphlets.

Public High School Library, Long Island City, N. Y. Peter E. Demarest, Principal; Miss Emma W. Heermance, in charge of Library. 201

HISTORY.—School library; supported by taxation.

REGULATIONS.—Open 8.30 A. M.–4 P. M.; reference and circulating; privileges restricted to members of the School.

RESOURCES.—About 1500 vols.

Public High School Library, Port Richmond, Heberton Avenue, Port Richmond, S. I., N. Y. Eugene G. Putnam, Principal. 202

HISTORY.—School library; supported by taxation.

REGULATIONS.—Open 200 days in the year; 2 hours a week for circulation and 35 hours for reference; free for reference; circulating privileges enjoyed by members of the higher grades of the School.

RESOURCES.—1384 vols.

Public Library. *See* New York Public Library; Astor, Lenox, and Tilden Foundations.

* **Public School Library,** Maspeth, L. I., N. Y. Miss Fanny West, in charge. 203

HISTORY.—School library; supported by taxation; free to the public; income for 1900, $94.

REGULATIONS.—Reference and circulating.

RESOURCES.—1298 vols. and 57 pamphlets.

Public School No. 15, Tompkinsville, S. I., N. Y. William A. Crane, Principal. 204

HISTORY.—Founded about 1866, formerly the library of School District No. 1 of the town of Middletown; school library; supported by public moneys.

REGULATIONS.—Open 8.30 A. M.–3.30 P. M.; reference and circulating; privileges enjoyed by teachers and pupils only.

RESOURCES.—1034 vols.

Public School No. 44. *See* Rockaway Beach Public School Library, No. 44.

Public School No. 72. *See* Borough of Queens Library.

Public School No. 87, Peck Memorial Library, cor. West 77th Street and Amsterdam Avenue, New York City. Edward Havemeyer Boyer, Principal. 205

HISTORY.—Founded 1893; school library; purchased by money raised by subscription and supported by public moneys and a small legacy left by a pupil of the school, Frederick Wright Peck, who died at the age of thirteen years.

REGULATIONS.—Open 9 A. M.–3 P. M.; reference and circulating; privileges enjoyed by pupils of school only.

RESOURCES.—About 3000 vols.

Public School No. 99, Throggs Neck, Borough of the Bronx, New York City. Bernard H. Kelly, B. S., Librarian. 206

HISTORY.—Founded 1858; school library; supported from public moneys; income averages about $30 a year.

REGULATIONS.—Open 8.30 A. M.–3.30 P. M.; circulating library; privileges restricted to pupils only.

RESOURCES.—About 1800 vols.

Public School No. 119, Flatbush Avenue, near Kings Highway, Brooklyn, N. Y. Moses Becker, Jr., Principal. 207

HISTORY.—Founded 18—; free school library; supported by public money; income for 1900 about $12.

REGULATIONS.—Open 42 days in the year; 1 hour each week for circulation; reference and circulating; privileges enjoyed by residents in school district or vicinity.

RESOURCES.—1060 vols. and 50 pamphlets.

Queens Borough Library, Nelson Branch (and Librarian's Office), 101 East Avenue, Long Island City, N. Y. Miss Jessie F. Hume, Librarian. 208

HISTORY.—Founded March 19, 1896; free public library; income for 1900, $5500. The Library has the following Branches: NELSON BRANCH, 101 East Avenue, founded 1896, 9990 vols.; STEINWAY BRANCH, 876 Albert Street, founded 1897, 4459 vols.; HOLLIS BRANCH, cor. of Fulton and Woodhull Avenues, founded 1897, received as a branch January 1, 1901, 1789 vols.; OZONE PARK BRANCH, Broadway, Ozone Park, founded 1897, received as a branch January 1, 1901, 917 vols.; RICHMOND HILL BRANCH, cor. Jefferson and Jamaica Avenues, founded 1899 received as a branch January 1, 1901, 3136 vols.; ASTORIA BRANCH, 112 Fulton Avenue, founded 1899, 2403 vols.; and QUEENS BRANCH, Railroad Avenue, founded 1899, received as a branch January 1, 1901, 1074 vols. Brief Historical notice of the founding, etc., in printed catalogue, and also in *Long Island Star*, March, 30, 1901.

REGULATIONS.—Open as follows: NELSON BRANCH, 9 A. M.–9 P. M. daily except Sundays and holidays; STEINWAY BRANCH, 9 A. M.–5 P. M.

on Mondays, Tuesdays, Thursdays, and Saturdays; HOLLIS BRANCH, 1–9 P. M. Tuesdays and Saturdays, and 9 A. M.–5 P. M. on Thursdays; OZONE PARK BRANCH, 1–9 P. M. on Tuesdays, Thursdays, and Saturdays; RICHMOND HILL BRANCH, 2–9 P. M. on Mondays, Wednesdays, and Saturdays, and from 10 A. M–6 P. M. on Tuesdays, Thursdays, and Fridays; ASTORIA BRANCH, 1–9 P. M. daily except Sundays and holidays; QUEENS BRANCH, 9 A. M.–5 P. M. on Mondays and Wednesdays, and from 1–9 P. M. on Fridays. ALL BRANCHES are open from 9–11 A. M. on holidays; reference and circulating; any resident of the city of New York can have the privileges of the library on application, others on payment of $1 a year; seldom interchanges books with other libraries.

RESOURCES.—23,778 vols. (distributed as shown above) and 300 pamphlets, not catalogued.

Queens Branch, Queens Borough Library. *See* Queens Borough Library.

HISTORY.—Formerly an independent library, founded in 1899; it was received into the Queens Borough Library, January 1, 1901.

* **Queens Free Library,** Queens, L. I., N. Y. Belle K. Hendrickson, in charge. 209

HISTORY.—Founded 1899.

REGULATIONS.—Open 156 days in the year; 7 hours each week for reference and circulation; free to the public.

RESOURCES.—433 vols.

Railroad Men's Branch of the Young Men's Christian Association Library, 361 Madison Avenue, cor. 45th Street, New York City. Wilbert Lovell McKinlay, Acting Librarian. 210

HISTORY.—Founded 1887; institutional library; supported by endowment and dues; income for 1900, $1758.54.

REGULATIONS.—Open 8.30 A.M.–9 P.M., Sundays, 1–6 P. M.; reference and circulating; privileges secured by membership; employés of any railroad terminating in the Grand Central Station or who are connected with some affiliated company are eligible for membership.

RESOURCES.—About 9460 vols.; works on *Railroads*, 848 vols.

Randall's Island House of Refuge. *See* House of Refuge, Randall's Island.

* **Rayson's (Misses) School Library,** 176–180 West 75th Street, New York City. Miss Amy Rayson, Principal. 211

HISTORY.—Founded 1895; school library; supported by School.

REGULATIONS.—Reference only; free to members of School.

RESOURCES.—1300 vols.

Reform Club, 233 Fifth Avenue, New York City. Walter T. Stephenson, Librarian. 212

HISTORY.—Founded 1888; club library; supported by occasional appropriations and gifts.

REGULATIONS.—Hours of opening correspond with club hours; reference and circulating; privileges accorded only to members of the Club.

RESOURCES.—About 10,000 vols.; specialties: *Political Economy* and *History*.

Richmond Hill Branch, Queens Borough Library. *See* Queens Borough Library. 213

HISTORY.—Formerly an independent library, founded in 1899; it was received into the Queens Borough Library, January 1, 1901.

* **Riverdale Library,** Riverdale Avenue, Riverdale, New York City. Francis H. Thorn, Librarian. 214

HISTORY.—Founded 1885; free library; supported by organization; income for 1900, $874.

REGULATIONS.—Open Mondays, Tuesdays, Thursdays, and Saturdays, 8 A. M.–10 P. M.; on Wednesdays and Fridays, 2–4 P. M.; circulating library; free to public.

RESOURCES.—About 2000 vols. and 50 pamphlets.

Riverside Branch, New York Public Library. *See* New York Public Library; Astor, Lenox, and Tilden Foundations.

HISTORY.—Formerly an independent library, founded in 1894 by the Riverside Association and turned over to the New York Free Circulating Library in 1897.

Rockaway Beach Public School Library, No. 44, Boulevard and Academy Avenue, Rockaway Beach, L. I., N. Y. William M. Gilmore, Principal. 215

HISTORY.—Founded 1893; school library; supported by public moneys, income for 1901, $45.71; free to pupils of School.

REGULATIONS.—Open 176 days in the year; 2½ hours each week for circulation.

RESOURCES.—680 vols.

Rosener Library. *See* Berkeley School; Rosener Library.

* **Round's (Miss) School Library,** 525 Clinton Avenue, Brooklyn, N. Y. Miss Christina Rounds, Librarian. 216

HISTORY.—Founded 18—; school library; supported by School.

REGULATIONS.—Reference and circulating; free to a limited class.

RESOURCES.—About 3000 vols.

* **Sacred Heart Academy Library,** Westchester, N. Y. Brother August, Librarian. 217

HISTORY.—Founded 1883; school library; supported by the Academy.

REGULATIONS.—Reference and circulating; free to members of the Academy; income for 1900, $300.

RESOURCES.—1200 vols. and about 1000 pamphlets.

Sailors' Library. *See* Cummings Library.

Sailors' Snug Harbor Library, New Brighton, Staten Island, N. Y. D. Delehanty, Governor, Sailors' Snug Harbor. 218

HISTORY.—Founded 1833; corporation library; supported by endowment.

REGULATIONS.—Open 8–10 A.M., 2–4 P.M.; reference and circulating.

RESOURCES.—About 4000 vols.

St. Agnes Branch, New York Public Library. *See* New York Public Library; Astor, Lenox, and Tilden Foundations.

HISTORY.—Formerly an independent free library, founded January, 1894; it was received into the New York Public Library; Astor, Lenox, and Tilden Foundations, July, 1901.

* **St. Agnes' Female Seminary,** 283 Union Street, Brooklyn, N. Y. Sister M. Celestine, in charge. 219

HISTORY.—Founded 18—.

REGULATIONS.—Free to a limited class.

RESOURCES.—850 vols.

* **St. Aloysius' Library,** 208 East 4th Street, New York City. Henry Jung, Librarian. 220

REGULATIONS.—Open Tuesdays and Thursdays, 7.30–9 P. M.

St. Barnabas' Free Reading Room, 38 Bleecker Street, New York City. Reuben A. Meyers, Librarian. 221

HISTORY.—Founded 1867; free to public; supported by the general funds of the New York Protestant Episcopal City Mission Society. Historical notice in Annual Report of the Society.

REGULATIONS.—Open 7 P. M.–10 P. M., excepting Sundays and holidays; reference only; free to all well-behaved men.

RESOURCES.—About 1100 vols.

* **St. Brigid's Academy School Library,** New York City. Sister Mary Leoiadia, in charge. 222

HISTORY.—Founded 1856.

REGULATIONS.—Open 200 days in the year; 6 hours each week for circulation; free to a limited class.

RESOURCES.—589 vols.

* **St. Francis College,** 300 Baltic Street, Brooklyn, N. Y. Robert Magner, in charge; Brother Paul, Secretary. 223

HISTORY.—Founded 1884; college library; supported by College; income for 1900, $100.

REGULATIONS.—Open 300 days in the year; 10 hours each week for reference and one half hour for circulation; free to a limited class.

RESOURCES.—4250 vols. and about 1100 pamphlets.

St. Francis Hospital Library, 609 Fifth Street, New York City. Sisters of the Poor of St. Francis, in charge. 224

HISTORY.—Founded 1865; institutional library.

REGULATIONS.—Open the entire day; used by patients of Hospital.

RESOURCES.—About 1085 vols.

* **St. Francis Xavier Academy,** 721 Carroll Street, Brooklyn, N. Y. Sister M. Borgia, in charge. 225

HISTORY.—Founded 1894.

REGULATIONS.—Open 40 days in the year; 2 hours each week for circulation; free to a limited class.

RESOURCES.—858 vols.

St. Francis Xavier, College of. *See* College of St. Francis Xavier, Faculty Library, *and* Students' Library.

* **St. Gabriel's Academy of Manhattan,** 233 East 36th Street, New York City. Sister M. Beatrice, in charge. 226

HISTORY.—Founded 1860; income for 1900, $40.

REGULATIONS.—Open 200 days in the year; 2 hours each week for circulation; free to a limited class.

RESOURCES.—866 vols.

St. Gabriel's Parish Library, 307 East 36th Street, New York City. Brother Michael, Principal. 227

HISTORY.—Founded 1894; educational library; supported by endowment; income for 1900, $28.14.

REGULATIONS.—Open from 3–4 P. M. on school days; reference library; only used by pupils in attendance.

RESOURCES.—514 vols. and 118 pamphlets.

St. George's Free Circulating Library, 207 East 16th Street, New York City. Miss Emma A. Bays, Librarian. 228

HISTORY.—Founded 1893; free society library; supported by occasional contributions; income for 1900, about $20.

REGULATIONS.—Open 4–5 P.M. Sundays, 7.30–9.30 P.M. Mondays, Wednesdays, and Fridays; circulating; privileges may be secured by joining one of the organizations of St. George's Church.

RESOURCES.—3350 vols.

* **St. James' Academy,** 64 Johnson Street, Brooklyn, N. Y. Sister Michaela, in charge. 229

HISTORY.—Founded 1869; income for 1900, $50.

REGULATIONS.—Open 200 days each year; 60 hours each week for reference and 30 hours for circulation; free to a limited class.

RESOURCES.—742 vols.

St. John's College, Fordham, 190th Street, New York City. Rev. Joseph I. Ziegler, S. J., Librarian. 230

HISTORY.—Founded 1841; educational library; supported by dues and private subscriptions.

REGULATIONS.—Open 12.30–1.30 P.M. daily; reference and circulating; privileges obtained by students on payment of dues.

RESOURCES.—About 40,000 vols. and 7300 pamphlets; *Art* and *Architecture*, 1200 vols.

* **St. John's College (Harnett Free Library),** Willoughby Avenue, cor. of Lewis, Brooklyn, N. Y. J. J. Sullivan in charge; Rev. Thomas F. Walsh, D.D., Ph.D., Librarian. 231

HISTORY.—Founded 1896; college library; supported by College; income for 1900, $233.

REGULATIONS.—Reference and circulating; free to a limited class.

RESOURCES.—About 3000 vols. and 150 pamphlets.

* **St. John's Orphan Home Library,** 922 St. Mark's Avenue, near Albany Avenue, Brooklyn, N. Y. Mother M. de Chantal, Superintendent. 232

HISTORY.—Founded 1870; asylum library; supported by the Home.

REGULATIONS.—Open 100 days each year, 2 hours each week for circulation; reference and circulating; free to inmates.

RESOURCES.—1060 vols. and 600 pamphlets.

St. Joseph's Academy, Flushing, Borough of Queens, N. Y. Sister of St. Joseph, Librarian. 233

HISTORY.—Founded 1874; educational library; supported by dues ($1 a year to those who wish to take out works of fiction); income for 1900, $200.

REGULATIONS.—Open 1 hour a week; reference and circulating; all inmates can have access to Encyclopedias, Historical and Poetical works.

RESOURCES.—About 3500 vols. and 100 pamphlets.

* **St. Lawrence Academy of Manhattan,** 42 East 84th Street, New York City. Sister Maria Consilio, in charge. 234

HISTORY.—Founded 1854.

REGULATIONS.—Free to a limited class.

RESOURCES.—645 vols.

St. Mark's Memorial Chapel Library. *See* Free Library of St. Mark's Memorial Chapel.

* **St. Mary's Cathedral School,** Garden City, L. I., N. Y. Miss Elizabeth L. Koues, Principal. 235

HISTORY.—Founded 1872; school library; supported by the School.

REGULATIONS.—Reference and circulating.

RESOURCES.—About 5000 vols.

St. Mary's School Library, 6–8 East 46th Street, New York City. Sisters of St. Mary, in charge. 236

St. Mary's School Library (*continued*).

HISTORY.—Founded 1890, in 1893 the Alumnæ Association gave $1000 for the purchase of books and an annual contribution of $25; school library; supported by school fund.

REGULATIONS.—Open 9 A. M.–6 P. M.; reference and circulation; free to a limited class.

RESOURCES.—About 3500 vols., 100 pamphlets, and about 4500 *Art Photographs* and *Engravings*, illustrating different schools of painting, sculpture, and architecture.

* **St. Nicholas Society Library,** 1286 Broadway, New York City.

HISTORY.—Founded 1835.

St. Paul's School Library, Garden City, L. I., N. Y. Horace E. Henderson, Librarian. 237

HISTORY.—Founded 1883; school library; supported by the School; in 1900 received a gift of $1000.

REGULATIONS.—Open during school hours; reference and circulating; privileges enjoyed by students only.

RESOURCES.—About 1500 vols.

* **St. Theresa's Ursuline Academy,** 139 Henry Street, New York City. Mother M. Lucy, Superior. 238

HISTORY.—Founded 1874; school library; supported by the Academy.

REGULATIONS.—Reference only; free to a limited class.

RESOURCES.—About 1000 vols.

St. Thomas Aquinas' Academy Library, cor. Ninth Street and Fourth Avenue, Brooklyn, N. Y. Sister M. Camilla, Librarian. 239

HISTORY.—Founded 1895; free school library; supported by the Academy.

REGULATIONS.—Open 9 A. M.–6 P. M.; reference only; privileges obtained by attending the School.

RESOURCES.—About 1500 vols. and 300 pamphlets.

Salmagundi Club Library, 14 West 12th Street, New York City, William Henry Shelton, Chairman of Library Committee. 240

HISTORY.—Founded 1890; club library; supported by the Club; income for 1900, $515.

REGULATIONS.—Reference only; free to members of the Club.

RESOURCES.—1631 vols. and pamphlets. Specialties: 128 volumes on *Costumes;* 35 works on *Gypsies* and 17 on the *Dauphin-Louis XVII*. The library is mostly composed of *Art Works*, technical or sumptuous catalogues, and books of reference.

Saratoga Branch, Brooklyn Public Library. *See* Brooklyn Public Library.

Schermerhorn Street Branch, Brooklyn Public Library. *See* Brooklyn Public Library.

HISTORY.—Formerly an independent library, founded 1866, by the Union for Christian Work; it was received into the Brooklyn Public Library, January 1, 1901.

Schirmer (G.) Circulating Library of Music, 35 Union Square, New York City. Gustav zur Nieden, Librarian. 241

HISTORY.—Founded 1876; subscription library.

REGULATIONS.—Open daily 8.30 A. M.–6 P. M.; privileges secured by taking a subscription; 3 months, $4; 6 month, $7; or $12 a year.

RESOURCES.—600 standard operas, 100 various collections, and 60,000 pieces of sheet music; specialties, *Standard Operas*, and *Classical and Modern Piano, Vocal, and Violin Compositions.*

School Library. *See* Public School Library; Union Free School Library; *and* Union School Library.

School No. 31, 200 Monroe Street, New York City. F. K. Montfort, Principal. 242

HISTORY.—School library; supported by public moneys; income for 1900, $25.00.

School No. 31 (*continued*).

REGULATIONS.—Open Fridays at 3 P.M.; reference and circulating free to pupils of School only.

RESOURCES.—About 300 vols.

Seaman's Free Library, 34 Pike Street, New York City. *See* Protestant Episcopal Church Missionary Society for Seamen.

Seamen's Friend Society, American. *See* American Seamen's Friend Society, 76 Wall Street.

Seamen's Library. *See* Cummings Library, 21 Coenties Slip.

Seamen's Reading Room. *See* Protestant Episcopal Church Missionary Society for Seamen.

Seventh Regiment Military Library, Seventh Regiment Armory, 67th Street and Park Avenue, New York City. James R. Mercien, Librarian. 243

HISTORY.—Founded 1860; regimental library; supported by regimental appropriations.

REGULATIONS.—Open 7.30–10 P. M., daily from October 1st to April 1st; circulating; privileges enjoyed by members of the regiment only.

RESOURCES.—About 7000 vols. and 500 pamphlets; about three-fifths of which are devoted to *Military Literature*.

Society for Ethical Culture, 48 East 58th Street, New York City. Henry G. Ives. 244

"We have no library in this building, but are accumulating a few books and magazines which may, in the future, be worthy of mention."

Society Library. *See* New York Society Library.

Society of the New Church. *See* Free Library and Reading Room of the Brooklyn Society of the New Church.

Sociological Reference Library. *See* Charity Organization Society Library.

South Brooklyn Branch, Brooklyn Public Library. *See* Brooklyn Public Library.

South Third Street Station, 754 Driggs Avenue, Brooklyn, N. Y. 245

REGULATIONS.—Open 7–9 P. M. on Tuesdays and Fridays.

* **Spalding Literary Union,** 34 West 60th Street, New York City. E. Francis Gordon, Librarian. 246

HISTORY.—Founded 1885; society library; supported by the Union.

REGULATIONS.—Reference only; free to members of the Union.

RESOURCES.—About 1000 vols.

Spence's (Miss) School Library, 6 West 48th Street, New York City. Miss Ella C. Williams, Librarian. 247

HISTORY.—Founded 1892; school library; supported by private funds.

REGULATIONS.—Open 8.30 A. M.–5.30 P. M.; reference and circulating; privileges enjoyed only by members of the School.

RESOURCES.—About 3000 vols.; has a branch at 26 West 55th Street.

Spicer Memorial Library of the Polytechnic Institute of Brooklyn, Livingston Street, near Court, Brooklyn, N. Y. Charles A. Green, A. M., Librarian. 248

HISTORY.—Founded 1891; educational library; supported by endowment.

REGULATIONS.—Open 9 A. M.–5 P. M., closed on Saturdays; reference and circulating; professors and students, only, enjoy its privileges.

RESOURCES.—About 7700 vols.

Staten Island Academy and Latin School Library. *See* Arthur Winter Memorial Library.

Steinway Branch. *See* Queens Borough Library.

Teachers College Library of the City of New York. *See* Bryson Library of the Teachers College of the City of New York.

Technischer Verein von New York, 192 Third Avenue, New York City. Leo Kiesler, Librarian. 249

HISTORY.—Founded 1875; society library.

REGULATIONS.—Open Thursdays from 8–10 P. M.; privileges accorded to members of the society.

RESOURCES.—About 1000 vols. and 500 pamphlets; devoted to *Architecture*.

Tenement House Chapter Library, 48 Henry Street, New York City. Miss May Childs Parsons, Librarian and Chairman of Library Committee. 250

HISTORY.—Founded 1891; free public library; supported by city appropriation and voluntary contributions; income for 1900, $1390.24.

REGULATIONS.—Open 2–6 P. M., except Sundays, 7–9 P. M. Mondays and Thursdays; reference and circulating; privileges secured by applying to the librarian in charge.

RESOURCES.—2283 vols.; specially interested in work in connection with the King's Daughters Settlement.

Thirty-Fourth Street Branch, New York Public Library. *See* New York Public Library; Astor, Lenox, and Tilden Foundations.

Tilden Trust. *See* New York Public Library; Astor, Lenox, and Tilden Foundations.

* **Tombs Library,** Franklin Street, corner of Pearl Street, New York City.

Tompkinsville Public School Library. *See* Public School No. 15.

Torrey Botanical Club Library. *See* New York Botanical Garden Library.

* **Tottenville Library Association,** Tottenville, S. I., N. Y. S. C. McCormick, in charge. 251

HISTORY.—Founded 1899; free library; supported by state aid and gifts; income for 1900, $603.09.

REGULATIONS.—Open 156 days in the year; 15 hours each week for reference and circulation.

RESOURCES.—828 vols.

Tottenville Public School Library, Public School Building, Tottenville, Staten Island, N. Y. N. J. Lowe, Principal. 252

HISTORY.—Founded 18—; school library; supported by public moneys and Regents' grant.

REGULATIONS.—Open one hour Fridays for giving out and receiving, and for reference during school hours; reference and circulating; privileges granted to students in the School.

RESOURCES.—About 2500 vols.

Trade School. *See* New York Trade School.

* **Training School for Teachers,** Brooklyn, N. Y. 253

HISTORY.—Founded 1885; school library; supported by public moneys.

REGULATIONS.—Reference and circulating; free to a limited class.

RESOURCES.—About 1500 vols.

Travelling Libraries. *See* American Seamen's Friend Society.

Travelling Libraries Department. *See* Aguilar Free Library *and* Brooklyn Public Library.

Travelling Libraries, New York Public Library. *See* New York Public Library; Astor, Lenox, and Tilden Foundations.

* **Trinity English and Classical School Library,** New Brighton, S. I., N. Y. A. Sloan, Librarian. 254

HISTORY.—School library; supported by the School.

REGULATIONS.—Reference and circulating; free for reference.

RESOURCES.—1800 vols.

Trow Library of Directories, 21 University Place, New York City. Trow Directory, Printing, and Bookbinding Company, Proprietors. 255

Founded 1873; public use for small fee; supported by annual purchase.

REGULATIONS.—Open 8 A. M.–5 P. M., except Sundays and holidays; single reference free; researches and copying 30 cents an hour.

RESOURCES.—450 directories; contains all *State, City, and Local Directories of the United States and Canada,* of latest date.

Turnverein Library. *See* New York Turnverein Library.

Typothetæ of the City of New York, 108 Fulton Street, New York City. Charles H. Cochrane, Librarian. 256

HISTORY.—Founded about 1890; club library; supported by dues and donations.

REGULATIONS.—Open 9 A. M.–5 P. M., every business day; chiefly reference, but also circulating; privileges granted to any respectable person to use library for reference, and upon presenting letter from a member to take out books.

RESOURCES.—About 2000 vols. and 1000 pamphlets; the library is devoted to *Printing* and the *Graphic Arts,* "and is probably the largest in the world devoted to this subject."

Union for Christian Work Library. *See* Brooklyn Public Library, Schermerhorn Street Branch.

* **Union Free School Library,** Maspeth, L. I., N. Y. 257

HISTORY.—School library; supported by taxation; free for reference.

REGULATIONS.—Reference and circulating.

RESOURCES.—3000 vols. and 200 pamphlets.

Union League Club Library, 1 East 39th Street, New York City. William Bradford Child, Librarian. 258

HISTORY.—Founded 1863; club library; supported by appropriation from dues; income for 1900, $3500.

Regulations.—Open 17 hours each day, or from 7.30 A. M.–12.30 the next night; reference only; privileges obtained by Club membership; does not interchange with other libraries.

Resources.—11,000 vols.; the only specialty is works on the *Civil War*, of which the library has about 700 vols.

* **Union School Library,** Hollis, L. I., N. Y. J. A. Loope, in charge. 259

History.—Free to a limited class.

Resources.—About 200 vols.

* **Union School Library,** Woodhaven, N. Y. C. E. Smith, in charge. 260

Regulations.—Open 190 days each year; 1 hour each week for circulation; free to a limited class.

Resources.—394 vols.

Union Settlement Library, 241 East 104th Street, near Second Avenue, New York City. Marion S. Morse, Librarian. 261

History.—Founded 1895; free public library; supported by state aid and dues; income for 1900, $212.

Regulations.—Open 1–6 P. M. two afternoons a week, Sundays and holidays excepted; reference and circulating; privileges secured by signing application and procuring a satisfactory reference.

Resources.—About 2000 vols.

Union Theological Seminary in the City of New York, 700 Park Avenue, between 69th and 70th Streets, New York City. Rev. Charles Ripley Gillett, D.D., Librarian. 262

History.—Founded 1836; educational library; supported by endowment; there are special endowments for the departments of Philosophy, British History and Theology, and American History and Theology; income for 1900, $4500. Historical notices : Prentiss, G. L., "Fifty Years of Union Theological Seminary"; also in his "Another Decade of Union Theological Seminary"; and in "Public Libraries in the U. S. A." (Wash., 1876), p. 153.

Union Theological Seminary (*continued*).

REGULATIONS.—Open 9 A. M.–10 P. M., except from 6–7 P. M.; reference and circulating; reference privileges are free to any respectable applicant, particularly if introduced by some person known to the librarian; circulating privileges granted to students and professors only; it interchanges books with other libraries.

RESOURCES.—74,385 vols. and 29,844 pamphlets; special features: *Incunabula*, about 400 vols.; *Hymnology*, over 5000 vols.; *Philosophy*, American, British, and Continental; *Westminster and Puritan Literature; Patristics; Roman Catholic Theology; Greek Texts of the New Testament; Periodicals;* in addition to the regular collections in all departments of Protestant Theology, making an actual total of over 75,000 vols. The total given is smaller because a large collection, not yet catalogued, is put down arbitrarily at a total of 5000. The pamphlet collection is actually about 40,000, the difference representing the uncatalogued pieces.

United States Engineer School Library and Museum, formerly at Willets Point, L. I., N. Y.

HISTORY.—This library has been removed to Washington Barracks, D. C.

United States Purchasing and Distributing Library for Ships of the U. S. Navy, Building No. 23, Navy Yard, Brooklyn, N. Y. Edward Preissig, Librarian. 263

HISTORY.—Founded 1890; government library; supported by naval appropriations.

REGULATIONS.—Office hours, 9 A. M.–4 P. M.; privileges obtained by personal application to the Equipment Office.

RESOURCES.—Stock on hand about 10,000 vols. About 16,000 volumes are purchased each year. The books on hand constitute the library for the use of the officers at the Navy Yard.

University Club, Fifth Avenue and 54th Street, New York City. William Henry Duncan, Jr., Librarian. 264

HISTORY.—Founded 1879; club library; supported by dues.

REGULATIONS.—Open 8 A. M.–2 A. M.; reference for members of the Club only.

Resources.—18,048 vols. Special features: 215 *Current American and Foreign Periodicals* on file; *Harvard Memorabilia*, 720 bound volumes; considered one of the best in the country, outside the Harvard University Library; *Princeton Collection*, 411 vols.; additions are constantly being made to both of these collections

University Law School. *See* New York University, Law School Library.

University Library. *See* New York University Library.

University Settlement Library, formerly **Neighborhood Guild Library,** 184 Eldridge Street, New York City. Miss Grace Louise Phillips, Librarian. 265

History.—Founded 1887; free to the public; supported mostly by public moneys; income for 1900, $4400.

Regulations.—Reading-Room open 9 A.M.–5.30 P.M., 7.30–9.30 P.M., Sundays, 1.30–6 P.M.; circulating department, 1.30–5.30 and 7.30–9.30 P.M.; privileges secured on application with a satisfactory reference.

Resources.—About 5000 vols.

Ursuline Convent Library. *See* Mount St. Ursula Academy Library.

Van Norman Institute, 122 West 70th Street.

* **Veltin's (Miss) School Library,** 160 West 74th Street, New York City. 266

History.—Founded 18—; school library; supported by the School.

Regulations.—Reference and circulation; free to members of the school.

Resources.—About 1000 vols.

Veterinary College Library. *See* New York American Veterinary College Library.

Veterinary College, New York American. *See* New York American Veterinary College Library.

Wadleigh High School. *See* Girls' High School Library.

Washington Heights Branch, New York Public Library. *See* New York Public Library; Astor, Lenox; and Tilden Foundations.

Washington Heights Free Library, 922 St. Nicholas Avenue, cor. West 156th Street, New York City. Edward P. Griffin, Librarian, Miss A. R. Van Hoevenberg, Assistant Librarian. 267

HISTORY.—Founded 1868; free to public; supported by public moneys, annual subscriptions, and gifts; income for 1900, about $7000, including an annual subscription of $1200 from Mrs. J. Hood Wright, used exclusively for books; became a branch of the New York Public Library, December 1, 1901.

Webb's Academy and Home for Ship-builders, Sedgwick Avenue and 188th Street, Borough of the Bronx, New York City. J. Irvin Chaffer, Resident Manager; Alexander H. Hidden, Librarian. 268

HISTORY.—Founded 1893; corporation library; supported by endowment and gifts.

REGULATIONS.—Open day and evening whenever books are desired; private library for use of inmates.

RESOURCES.—About 1400 vols. There is also a museum in connection with the Home containing models of vessels, paintings, pictures, and curios.

Webster Free Library, 526 East 76th Street, near East River, New York City. Edwin White Gaillard, Librarian. 269

HISTORY.—Founded 1892; free to the public; supported mainly by public moneys; income for 1900, $6223.99. Historical notice in "Evening Post," N. Y., June 2, 1900, also in "Annual Reports of the East Side House Settlement."

REGULATIONS.—Open for reference, 9 A. M.–10 P. M., and for circulation, 2.30–6, and 7.30–10 P. M., Sundays, 2.30–4 P. M.; privileges given upon an endorsed application; if signed by a teacher, applications are considered merely as recommendations and not as guaranteed; interchanges books with other libraries.

RESOURCES.—10,840 vols. and 200 pamphlets; Specialties.—*Bohemian literature*, 200 vols., largely translated; this library has a department of *Practical Illustration*, which lends to teachers timely picture bulletins and museum specimens, such as minerals, anatomical models, scientific instruments, and nature products in various stages of production, such as coffee, cotton, silk, etc. This department provides also photographs, colored pictures, and maps of various places and countries.

* **Weil's (Mrs. Matilda) School for Girls Library,** 109 and 111 West 77th Street, New York City. Mrs. Matilda Weil, in charge. 270

HISTORY.—Founded 1867; school library; supported by the School.

REGULATIONS.—Open daily, including Sundays; 10 hours each week for reference and circulation; free to a limited class.

RESOURCES.—About 2000 vols. and 500 pamphlets.

West Side Settlement, Young Women's Christian Association Free Circulating Library, 460 West 44th Street, New York City. Ada Laura Fairfield, Head Worker. 271

HISTORY.—Founded 1896; free to the public; supported by donations.

REGULATIONS.—Open from 3–9 P.M.; reference and circulating; privileges granted to applicants on recommendation of a business man.

RESOURCES.—3236 vols.; especially aims to encourage reading of children and has a great number and variety of books for children.

* **Westerleigh Collegiate Institute,** West New Brighton, S. I., N. Y. Amelia D. Allen, in charge. 272

HISTORY.—Founded 1894.

REGULATIONS.—Open 185 days in the year; 5 hours each week for circulation and 25 hours each week for reference; free to a limited class.

RESOURCES.—824 vols.

Williamsburg Branch, Brooklyn Public Library. *See* Brooklyn Public Library.

Woman's Library, 9 East 8th Street, New York City, M. J. Kemp, Superintendent. 273

Woman's Library (*continued*).

REGULATIONS.—Open 9 A. M.–4 P. M.

RESOURCES.—About 1500 vols.; any self-supporting woman with references can use the books of the library. This library is connected with the Working Women's Protective Union.

* **Women's Free Reading-Room and Library,** 16 Clinton Place, New York City. 273a

REGULATIONS.—Open daily.

* **Workhouse Library,** Blackwell's Island, New York City. John M. Fox, Warden. 274

HISTORY.—Founded 1876; asylum library; supported by public moneys.

REGULATIONS.—Reference and circulating; free to inmates.

RESOURCES.—1007 vols. and about 600 pamphlets.

Working Women's Protective Union. *See* Woman's Library.

Yacht Club Library. *See* New York Yacht Club.

Yorkville Branch, New York Public Library. *See* New York Public Library; Astor, Lenox, and Tilden Foundations.

Young Men's Benevolent Association Free Circulating Library, 311 East Broadway, New York City. Miss Helen Bernstein, Librarian. 275

HISTORY.—Founded in 1889 as a private library, made public in 1896; free to the public; supported by public moneys; income for 1900, $650.

REGULATIONS.—Open 4–9.30 P. M.; legal holidays, 6–9.30 P. M.; reference and circulation; privileges secured by written application endorsed by a member or business man.

RESOURCES.—About 4000 vols. and 500 pamphlets.

Young Men's Christian Association, 317 West 56th Street, New York City. Silas Hurd Berry, Librarian. 276

HISTORY.—Founded 1852; institutional library; free for reference; supported by endowment and dues; income for 1900, $10,350, and gift of $4700 for special purposes. This association has the following branches: 1. TWENTY-THIRD STREET BRANCH, 52 East 23d Street, cor. Fourth Avenue; 2. WEST SIDE BRANCH, 318 West 57th Street, near Eighth Avenue; 3. HARLEM BRANCH, 5 West 125th Street; 4. EAST SIDE BRANCH, 158 East 87th Street; 5. YOUNG MEN'S INSTITUTE, 222 Bowery, between Prince and Spring Streets ; 6. WASHINGTON HEIGHTS BRANCH, 531 West 155th Street; 7. STUDENTS' BRANCH, ("Students' Club" or "The Intercollegiate"), 129 Lexington Avenue; 8. SECOND AVENUE BRANCH, 142 Second Avenue; 9. FRENCH BRANCH, 49 West 24th Street; 10. ARMY BRANCHES, Governor's Island, Liberty Island, and Fort Wadsworth; 11. COLORED MEN'S BRANCH, 132 West 53d Street; 12. BOWERY BRANCH, 153 Bowery, corner of Broome Street; 13. RAILROAD MEN'S BRANCH, 361 Madison Avenue, cor. 45th Street; 14. RAILROAD MEN'S BRANCH, West 72d Street, cor. Eleventh Avenue; 15. RAILROAD MEN'S BRANCH, Melrose Junction, Yards, car 238 ; 16. RAILROAD MEN'S BRANCH, New Durham, Railroad Men's Building. Further particulars of Branches 1, 3–5, 7, 10, 13, and 14 will be found under their separate entries. Historical notice in "Association Notes," June, 1891, p. 61; "Public Libraries in the U. S. A." (Wash., 1876), p. 942–943. A "Catalogue of the Library: Circulating Department, July, 1900," has been published.

REGULATIONS.—Open 9 A. M.–10 P. M.; reference and circulating; reference privileges (open shelves) free to public; circulating privileges accorded to members only; Membership, $2 to $15; Life Membership, $100; the library interchanges books with other libraries.

RESOURCES.—About 45,000 vols. and 4000 pamphlets; Special features: *Architecture*, 912 vols.; *Art Antiquities*, 300 vols.; *Athletics and Out-door Sports*, 365 vols.; *Bibles* printed previous to 1700, 63 vols.; *Biblical Literature*, 2000 vols.; *Bibliography*, 750 vols.; *Birds*, 175 vols.; *Engraving and Examples*, many of these early scrap-book collections, 840 vols.; *Newspapers*, sets of N. Y. *Herald*, N. Y. *Times*, and *Tribune*, 675 vols.; *Patents and Specifications*, 950 vols.; *Periodicals, indexed in Poole*, 5750 vols.; *Portraits*, many of these unique scrap-books (one of 35 vols. containing more than 8000 portraits collected by John Perceval, Earl of Egmont, died in 1737), 204 vols.; *Sculpture*, 225 vols.; *Early Travels and Description*, 2500 vols.; *Waltoniana*, 94 vols. Boy's Department, 615 vols., circulated from 9 A. M.–9 P. M.

Young Men's Christian Association, Army Branch, Governor's Island, New York City. 277

HISTORY.—Founded 1899; association library; supported by Army Branch of the Association.

REGULATIONS. — Open 7.30 A. M.–9.30 P. M.; reference and circulating; free for consultation to soldiers; circulation among members of Army Branch of the Y. M. C. A.

RESOURCES.—350 vols. and loans from central library.

Young Men's Christian Association, East Side Branch, 158 East 87th Street, New York City. 278

HISTORY.—Founded 1884; association library; supported from branch budget; income for 1900, $24.47.

REGULATIONS. — Open 9 A. M.–10 P. M.; reference and circulating; free for reference to men; circulation restricted to members of Association.

RESOURCES.—1300 vols., of which 600 vols. belong to *Bible Study Library;* 300 vols. in Boy's Department.

Young Men's Christian Association, Harlem Branch, 5 West 125th Street, New York City. Frank G. Banister, Secretary. 279

HISTORY.—Founded 1868; institutional library; supported by membership dues; income for 1900, $225.

REGULATIONS.—Open 9 A. M.–10 P. M.; reference and circulating; privileges enjoyed by members of the Association.

RESOURCES.—3430 vols., of which 2780 are in main library and 650 in the Boys' Department.

Young Men's Christian Association, Seventy-second Street Railroad Branch, 72d Street, cor. Eleventh Avenue, New York City. 280

HISTORY.—Founded about 10 years since, had been previously at 30th Street; association library; supported by Branch.

REGULATIONS.—Open continuously night and day; reference and circulating; privileges restricted to members.

RESOURCES.—269 vols.

Young Men's Christian Association, Students' Branch, (" Students' Club " or " The Intercollegiate "), 129 Lexington Avenue, New York City. 281

HISTORY.—Founded about 1890; association library; supported by appropriations and donations; income for 1900, about $75.

REGULATIONS.—Open 7 A.M.–10 P.M.; reference only; privileges restricted to members.

RESOURCES.—360 vols. Specialty: works on *Christian Missions*.

Young Men's Christian Association, Twenty-third Street Branch, 52 East 23d Street, cor. Fourth Avenue, New York City. Werner Jonghaus, Associate Librarian. 282

HISTORY.—Founded 1852; institutional library; supported by endowment and dues.

REGULATIONS.—Open 8.30 A.M.–10 P.M., Sundays, 2–10 P.M.; reference only; free to all visitors.

RESOURCES.—About 10,500 vols. and 300 pamphlets; principally for use of medical and art students; *Medicine*, 700 vols.; *Art books*, 300 vols. Boy's Department, 730 vols., circulated from 9 A.M.–9 P.M.

Young Men's Christian Association, Various Other Libraries. *See* Brooklyn Young Men's Christian Association—Long Island Railroad Branch—Railroad Young Men's Christian Association Library—Young Men's Institute of the Young Men's Christian Association.

Young Men's Christian Union Library, cor. Westchester and Bergen Avenues, Borough of the Bronx, New York City. Harry Haffen, Librarian. 283

HISTORY.—Founded 1888; society library; supported by the Union.

REGULATIONS.—Open 7–10 P.M.; circulating library; privileges enjoyed by members of the Union.

RESOURCES.—About 1000 vols.

* **Young Men's Hebrew Association Library,** Lexington Avenue and 92d Street, New York City. Percival S. Marken, President. 284

Young Men's Hebrew Association Library (*continued*).

HISTORY.—Founded 1874; society library; supported by the Association; income for 1900, $1500.

REGULATIONS.—Reference only; free to members.

RESOURCES.—About 5000 vols.

Young Men's Institute of the Young Men's Christian Association, 222–224 Bowery, between Prince and Spring Streets, New York City. E. C. Baldwin, Secretary. 285

HISTORY.—Founded 1885; institutional library; supported by the Institute; income for 1900, $474.37.

REGULATIONS.—Open for circulation from 7–10 P. M., daily, except Sundays; for reference, 9 A. M.–10 P. M. on week-days, 2–10 P. M. on Sundays; privileges accorded only to members of the Institute.

RESOURCES.—About 900 vols.

* **Young Men's League Free Reading Rooms,** No. 131 Steuben Street, Brooklyn, N. Y.

* **Young Women's Association Library,** 33 Second Street, New York City. Miss Mary E. Underwood, Superintendent. 286

HISTORY.—Founded 1894; society library; supported by Association and public moneys; income for 1900, $152.

REGULATIONS.—Reference and circulating; free to the public.

RESOURCES.—1810 vols. and 3 pamphlets.

Young Women's Christian Association. *See* Harlem Young Women's Christian Association.

Young Women's Christian Association Free Circulating Library. *See* West Side Settlement.

Young Women's Christian Association of Brooklyn, Junction Schermerhorn Street and Flatbush Avenue, Brooklyn, N. Y. Miss Fanny D. Fish, Librarian. 287

HISTORY.—Founded 1888; institutional library; supported from funds of the Y. W. C. A., and special gifts; income for 1900, $1482.48. Historical notices in its printed reports.

REGULATIONS.—Open 9 A. M.–9.30 P. M., except Sundays and holidays; reference and circulating; privileges restricted to members of the Association; reading-room free to women; interchanges books with other libraries; circulates *Music* and *Art studies*.

RESOURCES.—10,100 vols.; strong in *Biography, United States History* and *Music*.

Young Women's Christian Association of the City of New York, 7 East 15th Street, New York City. Miss Harriet F. Husted, Librarian. 288

HISTORY.—Founded 1870; free to self-supporting women; supported by public moneys and dues; income for 1900, $6367.48.

REGULATIONS.—Open 9 A. M.–9.15 P. M., Sundays exclusive; reference and circulating; privileges obtained by presenting one city reference for reliability and character, and subscribing to rules.

RESOURCES.—28,920 vols.; Special features: *Music* and *Musical Literature*, 1000 vols.; works in *Foreign Languages*, chiefly French, German, Italian, and Spanish, 2000 vols.; *Art* and *Design* (including Mary Elizabeth Hoyt collection), 1000 vols.; *Education*, 400 vols.; *Domestic Science* and *Nursing*, 325 vols.; *Biblical literature* and *Missions*, 1800 vols.; also 654 *Art studies* and 57 *Cheer Pictures* (loaned to the sick).

INDEX
TO SPECIAL COLLECTIONS IN NEW YORK LIBRARIES.

The figures refer to the serial numbers of the libraries and not to the pages of the list.

When the subject is found, turn to the library indicated and see upon what conditions, if any, the collection is available.

It should be borne in mind that the larger libraries may have more volumes upon a given subject unreported than a smaller library which reports it.

In addition to books upon given subjects most libraries also have many pamphlets upon the same subject.

This Index does not claim to give a complete list of all the special subjects to be found in the libraries of New York, but only some of the most important ones.

MANUAL

AND

HISTORICAL SKETCH

NEW YORK LIBRARY CLUB

1902

1901—02

President.

Henry Marcus Leipziger.

Vice-Presidents.

Rev. Joseph H. McMahon. Minerva E. Grimm.

Secretaries.

Elizabeth Louisa Foote,
Silas Hurd Berry.

Treasurer.

Theresa Hitchler.

EXECUTIVE COMMITTEE.

Edwin White Gaillard,
Rev. Joseph H. McMahon,
Arthur Elmore Bostwick,
Helen Elizabeth Haines,
George Watson Cole,
Henry Marcus Leipziger, *ex-officio.*
Elizabeth Louisa Foote, *ex-officio,*
Silas Hurd Berry, *ex-officio.*
Theresa Hitchler, *ex-officio.*

MEMBERS OF THE EXECUTIVE COMMITTEE FROM THE ORGANIZATION OF THE CLUB.

BAKER, GEORGE HALL, 1888–94.
BALDWIN, ELIZABETH G., 1896–97.
BARDWELL, WILLIS ARTHUR, 1889–90, 1894–95, 1896–97.
BERRY, SILAS HURD, 1887–94, 1895–96, 1902.
BERRY, WILLIAM J. C., 1895–96.
BIGELOW, FRANK BARNA, 1900–01.
BILLINGS, DR. JOHN SHAW, 1897–1900.
BOSTWICK, ARTHUR ELMORE, 1896–99, 1901–02.
BOWKER, RICHARD ROGERS, 1885–88, 1889–90, 1894–95.
BURLINGHAM, CHARLES C., 1900–01.
CANFIELD, JAMES HULME, 1900–01.
CATTELL, SARAH W., 1895–96.
COE, ELLEN M., 1886–93, 1894–95.
COLE, GEORGE WATSON, 1891–95, 1901–02.
CRANDALL, MARY IMOGEN, 1890–92.
CUTLER, MARY SALOME, 1888–89.
DEWEY, MELVIL, 1885–86, 1888–89.
DEWEY, MRS. MELVIL, 1886–87.
DUNCAN, WILLIAM HENRY, JR., 1899–1900.
EAMES, WILBERFORCE, 1896–1901.
FOOTE, ELIZABETH LOUISA, 1900–02.
FORD, PAUL LEICESTER, 1889–91.
GAILLARD, EDWIN WHITE, 1901–02.
HAINES, HELEN ELIZABETH, 1901–02.

HANNAH, GEORGE, 1885–86.
HILL, FRANK PIERCE, 1886–87, 1888–89, 1890–94.
HITCHLER, THERESA, 1897–99, 1900–02.
HUSTED, HARRIET, 1899–1900.
IDLE, THOMAS WILLIAM, 1897–98.
KELSO, TESSA L., 1899–1900.
LEIPZIGER, HENRY MARCUS, 1895–96, 1897–1900, 1901–02.
LEIPZIGER, PAULINE, 1899–1900.
McMAHON, REV. JOSEPH H., 1900–02.
MERINGTON, MARGUERITE, 1887–89, 1895–96.
NELSON, CHARLES ALEXANDER, 1886–89, 1894–1901.
PEOPLES, WILLIAM THADDEUS, 1885–87, 1890–94.
PLUMMER, MARY WRIGHT, 1891–92, 1896–97.
POOLE, REUBEN BROOKS, 1886–88, 1889–95.
PRESCOTT, HARRIET BEARDSLEE, 1893–95.
RATHBONE, JOSEPHINE ADAMS, 1895–99.
SCHWARTZ, JACOB, 1885–88.
SMITH, BESSIE S., 1900–01.
STEVENS, WILLIAM FRANKLYN, 1895–96.
THOMAS, REV. JOSEPH CONABLE, 1895–96.
TUTTLE, ELIZABETH, 1892–97.
TYLER, ARTHUR WELLINGTON, 1887–89.
WEITENKAMPF, FRANK, 1898–99.
WING, JOSIAH NORRIS, 1899–1901.

OFFICERS
FROM THE ORGANIZATION OF THE CLUB.

1885–86.

President, Richard Rogers Bowker.
Vice-Presidents, Ellen M. Coe, William Augustus White.
Secretary, Charles Alexander Nelson.
Treasurer, Jacob Schwartz.

1886–87.

President, William Thaddeus Peoples.
Vice-Presidents, Frank Pierce Hill, Mrs. Melvil Dewey.
Secretary, Charles Alexander Nelson.
Treasurer, Jacob Schwartz.

1887–88.

President, Reuben Brooks Poole.
Vice-Presidents, Melvil Dewey, Marguerite Merington.
Secretary, Charles Alexander Nelson.
Treasurers, Jacob Schwartz, Silas Hurd Berry.

1888–89.

President, Melvil Dewey.
Vice-Presidents, George Hannah, Mary Salome Cutler.
Secretaries, Charles Alexander Nelson, Paul Leicester Ford.
Treasurer, Silas Hurd Berry.

OFFICERS

1889–90.

President, REUBEN BROOKS POOLE.
Vice-President, ELLEN M. COE.
Secretary, PAUL LEICESTER FORD.
Treasurer, SILAS HURD BERRY.

1890–91.

President, GEORGE HALL BAKER.
Vice-Presidents, { ELLEN M. COE, REUBEN BROOKS POOLE, FRANK PIERCE HILL.
Secretary, MARY IMOGEN CRANDALL.
Treasurer, SILAS HURD BERRY.

1891–92.

President, FRANK PIERCE HILL.
Vice-Presidents, { MARY WRIGHT PLUMMER, REUBEN BROOKS POOLE.
Secretaries, { MARY IMOGENE CRANDALL, GEORGE WATSON COLE.
Treasurer, SILAS HURD BERRY, *pro tem.*

1892–93.

President, SILAS HURD BERRY.
Vice-Presidents, { HENRY MARCUS LEIPZIGER, MARY C. MOSMAN.
Secretary, GEORGE WATSON COLE.
Treasurer, ELIZABETH TUTTLE.

1893–94.

President, GEORGE WATSON COLE.
Vice-Presidents, { HENRY MARCUS LEIPZIGER, FANNY HULL.
Secretary, HARRIET BEARDSLEE PRESCOTT.
Treasurer, ELIZABETH TUTTLE.

OFFICERS

1894–95.

President, CHARLES ALEXANDER NELSON.

Vice-Presidents, { WILLIS KIMBALL STETSON,
LILLIAN DENIO.

Secretary, HARRIET BEARDSLEE PRESCOTT.

Treasurer, ELIZABETH TUTTLE.

1895–96.

President, WILLIAM FRANKLYN STEVENS.

Vice-Presidents, { WILLIS ARTHUR BARDWELL,
ELIZABETH G. BALDWIN.

Secretary, JOSEPHINE ADAMS RATHBONE.

Treasurer, ELIZABETH TUTTLE.

1896–97.

President, MARY WRIGHT PLUMMER.

Vice-Presidents, { ARTHUR ELMORE BOSTWICK,
WILLIAM JAMES COURTNALD BERRY.

Secretary, JOSEPHINE ADAMS RATHBONE.

Treasurer, ELIZABETH TUTTLE.

1897–98.

President, ARTHUR ELMORE BOSTWICK.

Vice-Presidents, { WILBERFORCE EAMES,
HARRIET BEARDSLEE PRESCOTT.

Secretary, THOMAS WILLIAM IDLE.

Treasurer, THERESA HITCHLER.

1898–99.

President, ARTHUR ELMORE BOSTWICK.

Vice-Presidents, { WILBERFORCE EAMES,
HARRIET BEARDSLEY PRESCOTT.

Secretaries, { THOMAS WILLIAM IDLE,
FRANK WEITENKAMPF.

Treasurer, THERESA HITCHLER.

OFFICERS

1899–1900.

President, John Shaw Billings.

Vice-Presidents, { Frank Barna Bigelow,
Rev. Joseph Conable Thomas.

Secretaries, { Pauline Leipziger,
William Henry Duncan, Jr.

Treasurer, Harriet Husted.

1900–01.

President, Wilberforce Eames.

Vice-Presidents, { Henry Marcus Leipziger,
Elizabeth Louisa Foote.

Secretaries, { Bessie S. Smith,
Elizabeth Louisa Foote, *pro tem.*

Treasurer, Theresa Hitchler.

1901–02.

President, Henry Marcus Leipziger.

Vice-Presidents, { Rev. Joseph H. McMahon,
Minerva E. Grimm.

Secretaries, { Elizabeth Louisa Foote,
Silas Hurd Berry.

Treasurer, Theresa Hitchler.

CONSTITUTION.

I. Name.

This organization shall be called the New York Library Club.

II. Object.

Its object shall be to promote acquaintance and fraternal relations among librarians and those interested in library work ; and by consultation and coöperation to increase the usefulness, and advance the interests, of the libraries of New York and its vicinity.

III. Members.

Any person interested in library work and unanimously recommended for membership by the Executive Committee, may be elected at any meeting of this Club. Any library or any educational, social, industrial or similar institution or organization having a library or directly interested in library work and unanimously recommended by the Executive Committee, may be granted membership and representation at any meeting of this Club. All proposals for membership of either individuals or institutions, shall be referred to the Executive Committee and the Secretary of this Club shall keep a record of the person or persons making such proposals.

IV. Officers.

The officers of the Club shall be a *President*, two *Vice-Presidents*, a *Secretary*, and a *Treasurer*, who shall be elected by ballot annually at the regular meeting in May, and shall serve for one year from that time or until their successors are chosen.

The *President* shall preside at all meetings.

In the absence of the President, a *Vice-President* shall perform the duties of the office.

The *Secretary* shall keep a faithful record of all business transacted; shall give due notice of any election, appointment, meeting, or other business requiring the personal attention of any member; and shall have charge of the books, papers, and correspondence.

The *Treasurer* shall keep a full and accurate record of all receipts and disbursements and shall present a statement of accounts at each regular meeting of the Club, and an annual report at the annual meeting on the second Thursday in May. The Treasurer's account shall be closed on the 30th of April, which shall be the end of the fiscal year. He shall pay all bills against the Club after they have been certified by the chairman of the Executive Committee.

V. Executive Committee.

An Executive Committee of five shall be appointed by the President for the current year, to which the President, Secretary, and Treasurer shall be added as *ex-officio* members.

The first-named member shall be the chairman, and three members shall constitute a quorum.

It shall be the duty of the Committee to prepare questions for discussion by the Club; to consider and mature plans for the general work of the same; and to approve all bills before payment by the Treasurer.

The Executive Committee shall be empowered to spend money for the ordinary running expenses of the Club.

VI. Meetings.

There shall be regular meetings of the Club on the second Thursday of each October, November, January, March, and May, at such time and place as the Executive Committee may appoint.

The President shall call a special meeting of the Club on the written request of five members ; but notice shall be sent to each member not less than a week before such meeting.

VII. Dues.

There shall be annual dues of one dollar, payable at or before the November meeting, and a fee of one dollar at joining, which shall be in lieu of the annual dues for the current year.

The fiscal year of the Club shall begin May 1st.

No debt or obligation shall be contracted by any committee, officer or member of the Club on its behalf.

VIII. Amendments.

All amendments to the Constitution shall be referred to the Executive Committee, which shall report thereon, and the same may be adopted by a three-fourths vote at a regular meeting.

Notice to members before action on such amendments shall state that "Action will be taken on Amendments to the Constitution."

PUBLICATIONS OF THE CLUB.

Constitution and officers. 1885–86. Folder.

Constitution, officers, and members, 1886–87. Folder.

New York Library Club. Union list of periodicals currently received by the New York and Brooklyn Libraries. Edited at Columbia College Library. New York, 1887. 58 p. Q.

Officers and new members, 1887–88. Card.

New-York Library Club. Constitution, officers from the foundation, and list of members. New-York, New-York Library Club, April, 1891. 55 p. Tt.

Manual of the New-York Library Club. Officers, members, constitution, libraries represented, etc. New-York, July, 1894. 16 p. Sq. Tt.

New-York Library Club Manual. New-York, 1897. 31 p. D.

Libraries of Greater New York. Manual and Historical Sketch of the New York Library Club. New York, 1902. iv + 179 p. D.

PROCEEDINGS.

For reports of the proceedings of the Club to November 14, 1901, inclusive, see *The Library Journal*:—

Year.	Vol.	Page.
1885	10	148, 177, 178, 370, 400–402.
1886	11	3, 24–27, 67, 82–87, 145–146, 169, 341, 451, 484–486.
1887	12	74–78, 137–138, 164–166, 196–199, 250, 554–558.
1888	13	14–17, 98–102, 147–150, 217, 346, 381–382.
1889	14	42–44, 93–94, 416, 477–479.
1890	15	22–23, 116–117, 147–149, 212, 343–344.
1891	16	19–23, 51–53, 81–83, 115–118, 182–184, 281.
1892	17	25–27, 58–60, 98–100, 130–132, 204–207, 493–495.
1893	18	45–49, 86, 87, 158, 194–196, 515.
1894	19	20–22, 95–96, 133–134, 175, 386–387.
1895	20	95, 129, 212–214, 392–393.
1896	21	21, 24–27, 110–111, 153–154, 290–291, 509–510.
1897	22	33–37, 209–210, 266, 707, 756.
1898	23	112–114, 156–157, 250–251, 582, 630.
1899	24	29–30, 118–119, 161–163, 262, 636–637, 687.
1900	25	75–76, 126–130, 131–133, 297, 697–698.
1901	26	30–31, 219–220, 282–283, 759, 881–882.

PAPERS READ AND TOPICS DISCUSSED BEFORE THE CLUB.

Reference is made to the volume and page of *The Library Journal* in which the papers and discussions appeared. This record closes November 14, 1901.

Brooklyn Public Library and its plans for the future. *Arthur Elmore Bostwick.* 24: 636.

Bulletins and printed monthly lists. 18: 47–8.

Card catalog, The, of a great public library. *Dr. John Shaw Billings.* 26: 377–83.

Cards, Printing catalog, for libraries. 19: 20–2.

Catalog, A universal, of all printed books. *Thorvald Solberg.* 22: 210.

Catalogs, and the best mode of making known to the public the resources of a library. 17: 98–100.

Catalogs, What, shall we print? 13: 100–2.

Children, Methods of reference work for. *Mary Emogene Hazeltine.* 22: 112.

Children, The work for, in free libraries. *Mary Wright Plummer.* 22: 679–88, 707.

Children's library, The, in New York. *Emily S. Hannaway.* 12: 185–6.

Children's Library League of the Prendergast Library. *Mary Emogene Hazeltine.* 23: 114.

Children's reading, How can we induce parents to oversee their? *Edward Havemeyer Boyer.* 20: 22.

Citizenship, Help of libraries in training for. 20: 95.

Coöperation between free libraries and public schools. 25: 698.

Delivery stations or branch libraries. *George Watson Cole.* 17: 480–2, 493–5; 18: 45–7.

Denver Conference, Echoes from the. *Charles Alexander Nelson; Beatrice Winser.* 20: 392.

Dime-novel habit, What can be done to help a boy to like good books after he has fallen into the? *Ellen M. Coe.* 20: 22, 118–9.

Disinfection of books, The. *Dr. John Shaw Billings.* 22: 756.

Duplicates, Disposition of. 11: 87.

Early printed books, *see* Incunabula.

Endowment, On maintaining the public library by. *Mary Emogene Hazeltine.* 21: 26–7.

Fiction, popular, The St. Louis plan for meeting the demand for. *Frederick Morgan Crunden.* 25: 129.

—— System for, at Pratt Institute. *Mary Wright Plummer.* 25: 129.

Ford collection, The, in the New York Public Library. *Frank Weitenkampf.* 24: 636.

Home and club libraries. *Salome Cutler.* 21: 24.

Hours of library service. 24: 687.

Imprints, Early American. *William John James.* Pub. Weekly, May 19, 1900.

Incunabula in New York City. *Charles Alexander Nelson.* 24: 636.

Incunabula in the New York Public Library. *Wilberforce Eames.* 23: 251.

L. A. U. K. Conference at Southport. *Dr. John Shaw Billings.* 23: 582.

Lenox Library, The, and its founder. *Wilberforce Eames.* 23: 630; 24: 199–201.

Lenox Library — Its book treasures and art rarities. *Victor Hugo Paltsits.* 23: 630.

—— Its department of American genealogy and local history. *Charles D. Gillis.* 23: 630.

—— Its historical manuscripts and prints. *Harry Miller Lydenberg.* 23: 630.

—— Its map department. *Thomas Letts.* 23: 630.

HISTORICAL SKETCH.

By CHARLES ALEXANDER NELSON, A.M.

The NEW YORK LIBRARY CLUB was organized June 18, 1885, in the office of the Librarian of Columbia College, on 49th Street, by the persons named below, who met in response to the following call:

> "DEAR SIR,—Last year a meeting was proposed to discuss the desirability and practicability of an informal club of New York librarians, to hold six or eight meetings per year. There are many matters in which knowledge of each other's work and plans would result in coöperation greatly to our mutual advantage. It is certainly wise to have one meeting to see whether more are desirable.
>
> "Will you therefore meet us here Thursday, June 18th at 4 P.M., and invite any others in your library or outside who may be interested? Please try to be present or send word whether we may count you as interested.
>
> "This meeting is especially needed now to consider what may be done to interest any foreign librarians who come thro' New York to the meeting of the A. L. A. at Lake George in Sept."

The charter members were Henry M. Baird, D.D., Miss Ellen M. Coe, Max Cohen, Melvil Dewey, Mrs. Melvil Dewey, John MacMullen, Charles Alex. Nelson, Wm. Thaddeus Peoples, Reuben Brooks Poole, and Jacob Schwartz, of New York, and Wm. Augustus White and George Hannah, of Brooklyn. Seven others sent regrets for absence with expression of a wish to join. Wm. T. Peoples was chosen chairman and Melvil Dewey secretary of the meeting. It was decided to hold meetings of the Club in November, January, March, and May; a constitution was adopted and Messers. Dewey, Peoples, Bowker, Schwartz, and Hannah were chosen as Executive Committee.

The Executive Committee met on Friday evening, Sept. 11th, at the Sagamore, Lake George, and elected Richard Rogers Bowker, president, Miss Ellen M. Coe and Wm. A. White, vice-presidents, C. Alex. Nelson, secretary, and Jacob Schwartz, treasurer.

The first meeting of the Club was held Nov. 12th, 1885, at 3 P.M., at Columbia College Library. Forty persons were present. The topics considered were "Local coöperation of New York libraries in: *a.* A Union list of periodicals in these libraries; *b.* Inter-library loans and courtesies; *c.* Book thieves; *d.* Disposition of duplicates."

Messrs. Dewey, Nelson, and Schwartz were appointed a committee to prepare and submit a Union list of periodicals in the libraries of New York, to contain all indexed in Poole and all current periodicals and newspapers. Eight libraries voted to coöperate in the expense.

R. B. Poole, Miss Coe, and George Hannah were appointed a committee to report what steps could be taken to protect our libraries from book thieves and to present a plan for action. This Committee subsequently recommended that a secret list of the names of suspected persons be prepared for the use of librarians.

At the second meeting of the Club, held Jan. 14, 1886, thirty-one new members were elected. The topic discussed was "Free public libraries in New York City," and Reservoir Park, 5th Avenue and 42d Street, was proposed as a suitable site for a central library building. Messrs. Nelson, Schwartz, and Berry were appointed a committee to collect statistics and ascertain the specialties of the various libraries of New York and vicinity.

On the evening of Feb. 24th a special public meeting was held in the law lecture room at Columbia College. Eighty persons were present. Hon. Adolph L. Sanger spoke in behalf of the movement to incorporate the New York Library. A resolution was passed endorsing the Bill providing for its incorporation and appropriating $750,000 for the erection of a building. This Bill was killed in committee.

At the fourth meeting, held March 11, 1886, the Committee on book thieves reported a Bill amending the law relating to the mutilation of books. The Secretary read the Hendricks Act to encourage the growth of free circulating libraries. Under this Act a library circulating 75,000 volumes annually was to receive $5000, and the same amount for each additional 100,000 volumes, the total amount to any one library not to exceed $40,000.

At the meeting on May 13th the first volume of the new Astor Library Catalogue was exhibited, and a resolution was passed congratulating the Board of Trustees on its publication. A letter from Dr. H. A. Homes, the State librarian, was read in reference to his drafting a general library law for the State. On June 5th the Executive Committee authorized the Secretary to print copies of the Constitution and a full list of the members.

The proposed work of the A. L. A. Publishing Section was discussed at the November meeting held at Columbia College Library, and this led to the selection of "Highest legibility of type" as one topic for the next session, and "The libraries of New York and their relation to the public schools" was selected as another.

The Secretary was authorized to secure press clippings on library matters, which furnished a very valuable stock of information for subsequent meetings.

At the seventh meeting, Jan. 13, 1887, resolutions favoring a reduction of postage on library books were adopted. It was voted to make the March meeting an open one and the Executive Committee was requested to secure one or more essays on the "Relation of libraries to the public schools." At a special meeting held Feb. 10th the "Best size for a printed page" was discussed. On March 10th the public meeting was held at Columbia College, and Miss Marguerite Merington read a paper on "The relation of public libraries to public schools from a teacher's point of view," the first paper read to the Club. In the absence of Mr. Max Cohen, Mr. Dewey continued the discussion of the topic. On motion of Miss Merington, the Executive Committee was instructed to appoint a joint committee of librarians and teachers to formulate a line of coöperative work and lay the same before the Board of Education.

At the tenth meeting, on May 12th, the topic discussed was "What privileges do the libraries of New York extend to the teachers and scholars of the public schools?" A paper by Miss Emily S. Hannaway on "The Children's Library in New York" was read by Mr. Bowker. At the meeting held Nov. 10th, Mr. John Davies Mullins, librarian of the Birmingham (Eng.) Free Libraries, was present, addressed the Club, and was elected the first honorary member. The Committee on "Union list of periodicals" reported that the List was published and delivered to subscribers, the edition of one thousand copies costing $255.83. The death of Mr. John F. Sargent, librarian at Paterson, N. J., was announced, the first break in the membership of the Club from this cause. "The New York libraries and the subsidy question" was discussed; the Hendricks Library law was criticised and a committee was appointed to suggest amendments.

At the twelfth meeting, Jan. 12, 1888, the Committee on size of book page recommended 17½ by 25 cm. as the standard size for catalog and bulletin work, and postal size, 7½ by 12½ cm. for dodgers and small circulars. The recommendations were adopted. The topic discussed was "Library seminaries." At the March meeting amendments to the Library law were proposed, and, after discussion, were referred to Judge Howland, who subsequently reported unfavorably thereon. Book thieves were reported on and discussed. The topic "What catalogs shall we print?" called forth a quite free expression of opinions. The Secretary announced the preparation of a paper on "Library legislation," which would appear in Appleton's Annual for 1887.

The topics discussed at the May meeting, held at Columbia College, were "How best to stimulate the formation of public libraries in New York State," and "Should mercantile libraries be sustained independently or merged into free public libraries?" The Secretary reported that only seventeen responses had been received from public libraries in answer to forty inquiry blanks sent out by the Committee on library statistics. At the fifteenth meeting, Nov. 8th, Prof. H. Carrington Bolton, of Washington, D. C., gave an interesting talk on "Facilities afforded readers in European libraries." The treatment of pamphlets was also discussed.

C. Alex. Nelson and A. W. Tyler tendered their resignations as members on account of their going South to fill positions as librarians, the one at New Orleans and the other at Wilmington, Del. The resignations were accepted to take effect on their crossing Mason and Dixon's line. Paul Leicester Ford was elected secretary to fill the vacancy caused by the resignation of C. Alex. Nelson.

"Catalogs of portraits and pictures" and the "Disposition of pamphlets in libraries" were the subjects considered at the first meeting in 1889. On March 14th, at the seventeenth meeting, Mr. W. E. Foster, of Providence, was present and took part in the discussion of the question "How far should reading be controlled in libraries?" No records appear of any meeting in May, and probably none was held, as, at the meeting of November 14th, held at the Brooklyn Library, the Treasurer made his annual report and the Executive Committee for 1889–90 was elected. "Periodicals in reading-rooms and libraries" was the topic considered. The Club examined the Brooklyn Library, visited the Long Island Historical Society, and were entertained by Mr. Gordon L. Ford in his fine private library.

January 9, 1890, the Club held its nineteenth session at Newark, N. J., with forty members in attendance. Mr. Paul Leicester Ford read a paper on "The differentiation or specialization of New York libraries," which was followed by a valuable discussion, and a collation.

The March meeting was held at the Astor Library. Miss Ellen M. Coe read a paper on "Should American literature be specially favored in our libraries?" An interesting discussion followed, and the Club then examined the Library.

At the twenty-first meeting, held May 8, 1890, at the Bruce Memorial Library, the subject of "Bookbinding" was taken up and considered. A committee of five was appointed to report on A list of the public and semi-public libraries of the city, and the probable cost of its publication. An outline of a circular asking information for the compilation of the Manual was published in the *Library Journal*, 15 : 212.

The Executive Committee, Oct. 16, 1890, revised the Constitution and met several times before the regular meeting which was held at Pratt Institute, Nov. 13, 1890. One hundred members and guests were present. The proposed Manual received considerable attention. "Reports of library news and items of interest from libraries represented" gave a pleasing variety and made an enjoyable meeting. The Institute was inspected with great satisfaction, and the Club was entertained by Mr. Bowker at his home.

The twenty-third meeting was held at the Union Theological Seminary. The new Constitution was reported by the Executive Committee, and a total membership of one hundred and ten announced. Mr. Gillett gave a sketch of the history and administration of the Seminary Library. The members inspected the Seminary and its library.

The twenty-fourth, a special meeting, was held Feb. 22, 1891, at the Hall of the Long Island Historical Society, Brooklyn. The Club was welcomed by the Rev. Dr. Storrs, president of the Society. The new Constitution was adopted. Dr. E. C. Richardson, of Princeton, read a paper on "The science of books." Mr. Lindsay Swift, of the Massachusetts Library Club, and T. L. Montgomery, of Philadelphia, reported respectively on the chilliness of the Boston atmosphere and the abnormal warmth of that of Philadelphia. Connecticut and New Jersey were also heard from. An assessment of fifty cents on each member was voted. After the meeting the members inspected the library and museum.

March 12th the Club met at the Railroad Men's Branch of the Y. M. C. A., and listened to an "Account of the libraries for railway employees," given by G. A. Warburton, secretary of the Railroad Men's Branch of the Y. M. C. A. Miss M. I. Crandall read a paper on "The duties of a library to its staff," which drew out a warm discussion.

The annual meeting was held May 14th, at Columbia College Library, where the Club was welcomed by President Seth Low in a brief and cordial address. About eighty members were in attendance. Miss Mary C. Mosman read a paper on "Methods of the Reference Department of the Pratt Institute Library"; William B. Child, of Columbia College Library, one on "The reference work of a college library," and the Secretary read a paper on "Methods of the Brooklyn Library," prepared by Willis A. Bardwell, its librarian. These papers brought out an interesting line of inquiry and remark on reference work in libraries. At the close of the meeting a collation was supplied by the Columbia College Library staff, which added a very pleasant social feature to the meeting, and promoted "acquaintance and fraternal relations" among the members present. Ex-Secretary C. Alex. Nelson was present as a guest.

The twenty-seventh meeting was held November 12, 1891, at Jersey City. The Club was welcomed by Dr. L. J. Gordon, president of the Trustees of the Jersey City Public Library, who made some humorous criticisms on the Dewey classification. Miss Mary W. Plummer read a paper describing the more notable features of the libraries visited by the members of the American Library Association on their trip to San Francisco. A collation was served and a very pleasant social hour was enjoyed after the meeting.

January 14, 1892, the Club met at the Mercantile Library. The resignation of Miss Mary I. Crandall, as secretary, was received in consequence of her having accepted a position in the Newberry Library, Chicago. Mr. George Watson Cole was requested to act as secretary for the remainder of the year. Mr. S. H. Scudder exhibited some photographic views taken during the California trip of the A. L. A. in October, 1891. A resolution was passed congratulating the Chicago Library Club on its organization. After a full discussion of the topics "Admission to shelves" and the "Use of costly and rare books," a collation was served. In February the Club again went to Brooklyn, meeting at the Y. M. C. A. Library. The Executive Committee reported the adoption of the rule that "If members of the Club fail to pay their dues after two years, notices having been regularly sent to them by the Treasurer, their names shall be dropped from the list of membership." The subjects considered were "Catalogs" and "The best mode of making known to the public the resources of a library." Mr. Stetson opened the discussion with a brief paper, and many members took part. Mr. Peoples announced an exhibition of illustrated books at the Mercantile Library.

The thirtieth meeting of the Club was held March 10, 1892, at the Young Women's Christian Association, 7 East 15th Street. Attention was called to the Bill before

Congress providing for the printing and distribution of public documents. The proposed law was quite fully discussed and its provisions met with general approval. Mr. Geo. H. Baker made the opening remarks on the topic "Library development in New York City," followed by Miss Coe, Mr. Peoples, Dr. Leipziger, and others. H. J. Carr, treasurer of the A. L. A., was present, and took part in the discussions.

The seventh annual meeting was held in May at Columbia College Library. The Library School was represented by Miss M. S. Cutler and the members of the Junior Class. Miss Ellen M. Coe read a paper on "The relation of libraries to public schools." A. L. Peck, of Gloversville, N. Y., being called upon, related his experience with the scholars and teachers of his city, with whom he had plenty of time to labor in person. Dr. Leipziger and President Hill advocated making renewed efforts to interest the school teachers in the libraries. Dr. Henry M. Leipziger, Miss Ellen M. Coe, and Miss Mary W. Plummer were appointed a committee to secure a joint meeting of teachers and librarians to discuss this question. W. T. Peoples opened the discussion of the second topic, "The equalization of the postage rates on books of all classes." After some debate a strong resolution was passed endorsing the House Bill providing for a change in the postal laws. The officers for the ensuing year were elected. After adjourning, a collation was served by the ladies of the Library staff.

The thirty-second meeting was held Nov. 10th at the Union for Christian Work, Brooklyn. Mr. Robert Foster gave an account of the Union, which had its origin in a small reading-room twenty-six years earlier. Mr. Bardwell introduced the topic of the day, "The best method of getting books into the hands of the people through branches and delivery stations." George Watson Cole followed with a paper on "Delivery stations or branch libraries." Mr. Samuel H. Ranck, of the Enoch Pratt Library, Baltimore, was present, and took part in the discussion. The day was stormy and the attendance was small. Ten questions were found in the question-box, the answers to which taxed the wit and wisdom of those present.

January 12, 1894, the Club met at Columbia College Library; about twenty members were present. The subject of "Delivery stations or branches" was again taken up, and Mr. Peoples gave his views. Mr. H. J. Carr, of Scranton, was present, and joined in the discussion, as did also A. W. Tyler. The second topic, "Printed bulletins and monthly lists," drew forth valuable statements of experience. The ghost of the Handbook again arose but was quietly laid.

The thirty-fourth meeting was held Feb. 9th, at the Y. M. C. A. rooms, 23d Street and Fourth Avenue. Mr. R. B. Poole read a valuable paper on "The Manuscript age," and numerous examples of mss. and facsimiles were passed for inspection. Mr. Tyler added remarks based on a twenty years' study of the subject. A letter from Dr. H. M. Leipziger, explaining the delay in arranging for a meeting of teachers and librarians, was read.

The March meeting was held on the 9th, at the Astor Library. Owing to a severe storm, only about twenty-five members were present. Mr. Tyler read a paper on "Books and bookmaking before the age of printing." It was illustrated by numerous specimens of mss. kindly brought together by Mr. Frederic Saunders, the librarian.

The custom of holding the annual meeting at Columbia College Library was kept up, and the Club met there on May 11th. Mr. Cole spoke on the first topic, "The Library School at Albany." In the absence of F. P. Hill, the President (Silas H. Berry) reported on "The Library exhibit at Chicago," giving a condensed account of it. The third subject, "Rebinding for general circulation," was discussed by Messrs. Baker, Poole, Cole, Tyler, Berry, and Miss Hull; their remarks were printed as a symposium in the *Lib. Jour.*, 18 : 186–7. Dr. Leipziger reported that Miss Coe and himself had met ten school principals on April 12th, at a two hours' meeting, in which all were much interested. Samples of the Rudolph Index with photographs were shown. George Watson Cole was elected president and Harriet E. Prescott secretary for the ensuing year.

At the thirty-seventh meeting, held Nov. 9th, at the Y. M. C. A. rooms, Dr. W. C. Prime gave a talk on "Early illustration of books by wood-cuts." Dr. Prime held the close attention of the members for over an hour, talking as freely and familiarly as though in his own library, and presenting much valuable information. By special invitation, after adjournment, the members went directly to the Grolier Club and inspected the exhibition of fine bindings brought from the World's Fair.

The session held Jan. 11, 1894, at the Mercantile Library, was mainly given up to listening to the plans for "Printing catalog cards for libraries," proposed by the Library Bureau and the Rudolph Indexer Co. Mr. Spencer E. Carr represented the latter and Mr. F. R. Fletcher the former. A full statement of what each proposed to do was made, and many questions were asked in reference to the form, style, and price of the proposed cards. A committee was appointed to wait upon Mr. T. L. De Vinne and request him to deliver an address at the next meeting on "Early printed books."

The thirty-ninth meeting was held Feb. 8th at Columbia University Library. The topic discussed was "Library statistics," and, from the remarks made, there appeared to be little uniformity, not only in the methods of keeping records of the use of books in libraries, but also of reporting the number of volumes and pamphlets they contained.

The meeting, on March 8th was held at the Railroad Men's Branch of the Y. M. C. A. Topic, "Reports of recent work and development and present condition of the several libraries represented in the Club." Mr. and Mrs. Henry J. Carr, of Scranton, were present, and Mr. Carr reported on new library work carried out in Philadelphia. Mr. Geo. H. Baker spoke of the rearrangement of the library of Columbia in the new building, withdrawing largely free access to the shelves; he announced a donation by President Low of the books illustrative of the German universities exhibited at the World's Fair, the printing of the Catalog of the Avery Architectural Library, and an anonymous gift of $20,000 to the Library. Resolutions were adopted on the death of Dr. William Frederick Poole, of Chicago, and several members gave personal recollections of Dr. Poole's high character and ability as a librarian. C. Alex. Nelson read a short poem* commemorating the completion of The "A. L. A." Library Catalog.

May 10th the Club met at Columbia University Library. A paper on "Special international bibliographies" was

* Printed in the *Library Journal* (1894) 19 : 134.

read by Mr. Axsel G. S. Josephson. Discussion on the topic, "What is needed in American bibliography," was opened by Mr. Bowker, who outlined the purpose and scope of the proposed American Catalogue of books from 1800 to 1876 not included in the 1876 volume of the "American Catalogue." The annual election of officers was held, and C. Alex. Nelson was elected president.

By special invitation from the Bryson Library, the Club held its forty-second meeting at the Teachers' College, Nov. 8th, and, though the day was stormy, about sixty members were present. President Walter Hervey, of the College, made a brief speech of welcome, and introduced Miss Grace Dodge, of the Board of Trustees, who spoke of the need of books in school work, of the way in which Mrs. Bryson had provided for the College, and of the need of coöperation between librarians and the teachers who seem to know nothing about books, nor how to bring them to the child. The discussion of the subject "How teachers should coöperate with librarians," was opened with the reading of a paper by Mr. Geo. W. Cole. President Nelson called attention to the fact that at five previous meetings the same subject had been before the Club for consideration. Mr. Poole, Mr. Baker, Miss Merington, and others, took part in the discussion, which emphasized the necessity of acquainting teachers with the willingness of librarians to aid them, and of interesting them in the selection of books for their children. A vote of thanks was passed to the officers and teachers of the College for their courtesy and for the social entertainment which followed the meeting.

The New York [State] Library Association and the Club united in a joint meeting on Jan. 11–12, 1895, at the

Y. M. C. A. rooms on 23d Street. Mr. R. B. Poole, president of the State Association, delivered an address on "The personality of the librarian," at 3 P. M., on the 11th. This was followed by a paper on "The library work of the University of the State of New York," by Rev. W. R. Eastman, superintendent of this work. Mr. A. L. Peck, of Gloversville, read a suggestive paper on "The adaptation of libraries to local needs," which reflected something of the admirable work done in Gloversville in the solution of the problem there. "The value of a classified arrangement of books" was considered in papers by Miss Jenny L. Christman, of Albany, Miss E. M. Coe and Miss Hitchler, of New York. Considerable informal discussion of the several papers helped to fill out a satisfactory program for the session.

"In the evening occurred one of the pleasantest gatherings of library people ever held in New York, the Library Club inviting the State Association and other guests to dinner at Clarke's parlors, on 23d Street. The menu was a triumph of President Nelson's skill in combining with the 'text' a 'gloss' of apt quotations, culled from writers ancient and modern." The leading after-dinner speakers were Dr. Edward Eggleston and Hamilton W. Mabie, and brief speeches were made by C. A. Cutter, W. I. Fletcher, R. R. Bowker, W. R. Eastman, and Geo. H. Baker. Miss Helen Moore gave a touching account of the University Settlement Library and its work. "The dinner was in every way a great success, valued perhaps as much for the delightful social intercourse afforded as for the more formal speaking."

The final session of the joint meeting was held Saturday morning, and was mainly devoted to the subject "Reading for the young," in answers to the three questions: 1. "How can we induce parents to oversee their children's reading," by Edward H. Boyer, a school principal of New York. 2. "How may we make the guiding of her pupil's reading a part of the teacher's work?" responded to by Miss Merington. J. C. Sickley, A. L. Peck, Miss Hewins, and others, contributed to the discussion which followed the paper. Miss Ellen S. Coe responded to question 3. "What can be done to help a boy to like good books after he has fallen into the dime-novel habit?" speaking hopefully on the whole, though admitting the difficulties in the way. Miss Mary S. Cutler discussed the "Principles of the selection of books" under three heads: Who shall select? What shall be chosen? How shall it be done? An interesting discussion ensued.

The forty-fourth meeting was held Feb. 15th at the Methodist Library. The subject discussed was "Help of libraries in training for citizenship," introduced by R. B. Poole. Rev. Dr. Thomas gave a full explanation of his method of shelving and preserving newspapers and periodicals in wrappers of manila rope paper. A pleasant hour was spent in inspecting the immense building of the Methodist Book Concern.

March 14th the Club met at the rooms of the Y. M. C. A. Geo. W. Cole read a paper on "Libraries of the twentieth century." The regular topic, "The proposed combination of the Astor, Lenox, and Tilden Foundations," elicited a full and interesting discussion, Messrs. Weeks (of Newark), Poole, Wing, Leipziger, Baker, Nelson, and Judge Peck, taking part.

The annual meeting was held at Columbia University Library May 9th. The death of Reuben Brooks Poole was announced; an appropriate minute was ordered spread upon the records and personal tributes were paid by the President, Dr. Leipziger, and George H. Baker. Resolutions were passed congratulating Columbia College on its magnificent gift from President Low for a library building. After electing officers for the ensuing year, the regular subject of the meeting was taken up, "The proposed bibliography of American literary periodicals." A letter from Professor H. Carrington Bolton was read and remarks were made by several members and by Mr. C. C. Soule, of Boston. Messrs. G. H. Baker and E. C. Richardson were added to the original committee, which was instructed to formulate a plan for a "General catalog of all American literary periodicals."

A committee of six with full powers was appointed to arrange for the celebration of the tenth anniversary of the founding of the Club, and $30.00 were appropriated towards the expenses.

At the forty-seventh meeting, held at the Mercantile Library, November 14th, the Committee on decennial celebration reported that it had been decided to celebrate at the annual dinner in January. It was voted to invite the State Association to join in the meeting and to be the guests of the Club at the dinner. C. Alex. Nelson read a paper, "Echoes from the Denver Conference," and Miss Winser reported on the "Experiences of four A. L. A. members on their trip to Salt Lake City." Reports on the second topic, "New work undertaken by the libraries represented during the past year," occupied the rest of the session. Some sixty members were in attendance.

The joint meeting of the State Association and the Club was held at the rooms of the Y. M. C. A., January 10, 1896.

Reference was made to the deaths of Ex-President R. B. Poole and of second Vice-President, Miss Louise S. Cutler. Miss Helen Moore read a paper on "Settlement libraries," Miss Mary S. Cutler one on "Home and club libraries," and Miss E. A. Bays one on "Parish libraries." A full and valuable discussion of these papers followed. Miss Hannah P. James presented a paper on "Librarians at the Atlanta Exposition." The morning session was closed by Miss Mary W. Plummer reading an account of the "New library building of the Pratt Institute," plans of which were exhibited. In the afternoon Mr. Henry S. Nourse, of the Mass. State Library Commission, made an address on "The State and the public library." Miss M. E. Hazeltine read a paper on "Maintaining the public library by endowment." J. M. Brandegee, W. R. Eastman, and Melvil Dewey took part in the discussion of the paper. Mrs. Nellie De G. Doubleday, of Bay Ridge, gave a full statement on "How to start a library movement." The question of the collation of books as received led up to an amusing and spirited discussion.

The tenth anniversary was celebrated by a dinner at Clarke's in the evening, attended by one hundred and twenty-five members and guests. Among the latter were Mrs. Ruth McEnery Stuart, the officers of the newly organized Brooklyn Public Library Association, Rossiter Johnson, Prof. F. W. Hooper, and Charles A. Cutter. The Rubinstein Ladies' Quartet, of Brooklyn, and Miss Gertrude J. Nelson, contributed the musical portion of the entertainment. The after-dinner speeches were excellent, and letters of regret from Seth Low, Andrew Carnegie, W. D. Howells, E. C. Stedman, Judge Henry E. Howland, and others, were read.

The February meeting was held at the Grolier Club, the whole Club-house being open for inspection. The program was planned to harmonize with the attractions of the place. Miss Louise Both-Hendriksen, a member of the London Ex-Libris Society, read a paper on "Book-plates," or "Ex-libris," as she preferred to call them. Mr. Theodore L. De Vinne addressed the Club on the subject of "Fine printing." Mr. J. O. Wright criticised the A. L. A. standard book sizes, and was answered by Messrs. Bowker and Geo. H. Baker.

A furious storm on March 19th reduced the number in attendance at the fiftieth meeting to about thirty. Mr. Bostwick called attention to the fact that six years had passed since the Club had met at the Bruce Memorial Library. The report of the Committee on the annual dinner was presented, with the recommendation that the next dinner be in celebration of the twenty-first birthday of the *Library Journal*. Mr. R. R. Bowker opened the program with a paper on "Libraries and library problems in Greater New York." This was followed by a discussion as to the best site for the New York Public Library. The second topic, "Bookbinding," was introduced by Mr. Nelson, who read extracts from an essay on that subject presented before the Grolier Club by Mr. William Matthews. This was followed by a talk on temporary binding in manila rope paper, in which Messrs. Thomas and Berry took part, showing how cheaply and effectively this material could be used. Mr. Berry also showed specimens of the writing of the call number directly upon the book in black or white ink, a single coat of French varnish preventing the ink from smearing.

The annual meeting was held at the hall of the Young

Women's Christian Association, May 14th. The subject for the meeting was the "History of the organization and work of the Club from its beginning;" a paper giving a summary of all the meetings for the first ten years, the place where held, and the program of subjects discussed, was read by C. Alex. Nelson, one of the charter members. Officers were elected for the ensuing year.

The fifty-second meeting of the Club was held Nov. 12th, at the Pratt Institute Library, Brooklyn, about one hundred being present in spite of stormy weather. Dr. J. S. Billings extended an invitation to hold some future meeting at the Astor Library. A communication from Mr. Tillinghast was considered in which the Club was urged to undertake the preparation of the monthly lists of select fiction, published by the Massachusetts Club last year. Misses Hitchler, Haines, and Winser were appointed a committee to confer with the Massachusetts Club and the State Association in reference to the matter. A committee was also appointed to confer with the State Association in reference to the annual dinner. An amendment to the Constitution was proposed providing for the omission of the February meeting. A reception committee of seven was appointed to serve for one year. The regular program was then opened. C. Alex. Nelson gave a report on "The A. L. A. Conference at Cleveland," introducing extracts from Mr. Dana's opening address and from Mr. Larned's indictment of the newspaper press. Miss Haines read a graphic and entertaining account of "The Post-Conference excursion." The third topic, "What should librarians read?" was postponed for want of time.

The annual joint meeting of the Club and State Library

Association was held Jan. 14, 1897, in the Art Building, in Brooklyn, by invitation of the Brooklyn Public Library Association. An all-day program was provided. In the absence of Mr. Larned, president of the State Association, C. Alex. Nelson, vice-president, called the morning session to order and welcomed the members to Brooklyn. W. R. Eastman read a paper on "Library progress in the State of New York." Mr. Richard Jones, the Regent's literature inspector, delivered an address on "Literature clubs." A symposium was then held on "What should librarians read?" conducted by Geo. H. Baker, W. A. Bardwell, A. E. Bostwick, and Wilberforce Eames. Miss Cutler, Mr. Richardson, Mr. Dewey, and Mr. Cutter also took part in the discussion. Mr. Dewey then spoke on "The relations that should subsist between library associations and the National Educational Association." The afternoon session was devoted to the discussion and criticism of the "Best books of 1896." The classified list of 489 of the leading books of 1896, prepared at the New York State Library, was taken as the basis. Mr. Peoples presented his selection of Reference books. E. C. Richardson discussed the books on Philosophy, Ethics, and Religion. Natural Science and Useful Arts were reviewed by T. L. Montgomery. C. A. Cutter talked of the books on Fine Arts, laying down the principles to be observed in buying art books for public libraries. The thirty-five titles in Social Science were reviewed and analyzed by Prof. Franklin H. Giddings, of Columbia University, in a masterful way, and a number of valuable additions were suggested. Fiction was presented by Miss Helen E. Haines, Literature by Miss Mary L. Davis, and Travel by Miss Mary W. Plummer, of Pratt Institute. Miss M. S.

Cutler discussed Biography. History, which had been assigned to Mr. J. N. Larned, was omitted, and Miss Hewins gave one of her pleasant talks on the children's books of the year.

The annual dinner at the Clarendon was not up to the usual high social and enjoyable standard, being subordinated to and cut short by the evening mass-meeting in the Academy of Music, arranged by the Brooklyn Public Library Association, at which R. Ross Appleton, Ex-Mayor Boody, Andrew Carnegie, Dr. Richard S. Storrs, Father E. W. McCarthy, Frederick B. Pratt, and Melvil Dewey, were the speakers. At this meeting the names of the Trustees of the Brooklyn Public Library were first announced.

The March meeting was held in the Astor Library on the evening of the 11th. The Committee on the Massachusetts fiction lists reported that the Massachusetts Library Club had decided to continue the lists, but asked for financial coöperation, which the Committee recommended. Dr. G. E. Wire and Miss Josephine A. Rathbone were appointed to represent the Club at the meeting of the N. E. A., at Milwaukee, in July. The subject of the evening was "Some recent bibliographical projects." Dr. John S. Billings spoke of the plan for indexing scientific publications decided on at the International Conference held in London last July. Mr. Thorvald Solberg discussed the project of a universal catalog of all printed books.

A special meeting was held at Columbia University, March 23rd, to protest against the omission from the free list in the Dingley Tariff Bill of books and apparatus for the use of libraries and other educational institutions. Dr.

Billings, chairman of the committee appointed to take necessary action, reported resolutions reciting the previous tariff legislation on the subject and urging the restoration of the privileges heretofore accorded, which were adopted, and the Secretary was instructed to send copies to the secretaries of other library associations throughout the country, to the senators and congressmen from New York, and to the members of the Club. The committee, consisting of Dr. Billings and Messrs. Nelson and Bostwick, was continued with power.

The fifty-sixth meeting, and twelfth annual, was held at the Railroad Men's Branch of the Y. M. C. A., April 22nd. About two hundred persons were present, including the Vice-director and students of the New York State Library School. The Club voted an appropriation of twenty-five dollars for the W. F. Poole Memorial Fund. The first paper on the topic for the day, "The organization and management of library staffs," was presented by Mr. Wilberforce Eames, giving an account of the organization of the staff of the New York Public Library in the Astor and Lenox buildings. A paper by Frank P. Hill, read by Miss Winser, gave "The practical side of staff organization, the duties and responsibilities"; Miss Hitchler discussed "The personal relations between the librarian and staff," and Miss Davis, of Pratt Institute, set forth "A theory of library administration." The officers for the ensuing year were elected.

A meeting was held at the Teachers College, Oct. 14th. C. Alex. Nelson gave a brief account of the second "Philadelphia Conference of the A. L. A." Miss Mary W. Plummer read a paper on "Children's libraries." R. R. Bowker gave an informal but reminiscent and particularly interesting talk on the "Second International Conference of Librarians at London," and the post-conference trip. He specially noted the absence of English women and the presence of American women at the Conference. Five o'clock tea was served to those in attendance.

The November meeting was held on the 11th at the Jackson Square Branch of the New York Free Circulating Library. Dr. J. S. Billings opened an interesting and lively discussion on "The disinfection of books." Following this he exhibited the sketch plans of "The proposed Building for the New York Public Library," and explained all the features which have been carefully worked out with a view of making it the best equipped library building of its kind in the country.

The annual meeting of the Club and the State Association was held at the Y. M. C. A., 318 West 57th Street, Feb. 17, 1898. Mr. A. L. Peck, President of the State Association, made the opening address, and then called on W. R. Eastman for an account of the " Free lending libraries of New York City." Mr. Frank P. Hill gave an exhibition and explanation of the plans of "The new building for the Newark Public Library." Mr. A. E. Bostwick took up the next subject, the "Development of reference work in circulating libraries." Miss M. E. Hazeltine discussed "Methods of reference work for children." The topic proved so interesting that time for its consideration was extended, and H. M. Elmendorf, Miss Pratt, and Mrs. Elmendorf contributed to the discussion. In the absence of W. E. Foster, his paper on "Methods of reference work with artisans" was read by title.

Mr. Bostwick, President of the Club, presided at the

afternoon session when the subject, "Some recent experiments on access to shelves in free circulating libraries," was reported upon by W. K. Stetson, of New Haven, Miss A. E. Brown, and Miss Cragin, of the New York Free Circulating Library. Mr. Elmendorf read a paper on the experiment made in Buffalo of placing a selected library of 6700 volumes on open shelves, with free access to all. Additional books to the number of 4500 had been added. Mr. T. W. Idle read an account of "Mudie's Select Library," of London with which he was connected for many years.

Mr. W. R. Eastman presented for consideration the "Select list of the fifty books of 1897" which received the highest vote throughout the State. Two classes of the year's books were presented in detail. Fiction, by Miss Helen E. Haines, and Juveniles, by Miss Caroline M. Hewins. Miss M. E. Hazeltine described "The Children's Library League," of the Prendergast Library, of Jamestown. A committee on legislation was appointed, consisting of Dr. J. S. Billings, W. C. Morey (of Rochester), J. E. Brandegee (of Utica), A. L. Peck, and W. R. Eastman.

The annual dinner was served at the Sturtevant House, preceded by a social reception from 7 till 8 o'clock. After-dinner speeches were made by President Bostwick, George Haven Putnam, Rossiter Johnson, A. Van Name, W. I. Fletcher, and Mr. Tillinghast, of Cambridge, Mass. The musical feature of the evening was contributed by Miss Blenner, Miss Cox, and the Misses Holt.

The sixtieth meeting was held at the Pratt Institute Library, Brooklyn, on the afternoon of March 10th. An account of the "Music and the literature of music in the

New York Public Library," was read by Mr. Victor H. Paltsits, of that institution. T. W. Idle reported on the collection of works on music at Columbia. Mr. Willis A. Bardwell read a paper on "Music at the Brooklyn Library." Verbal reports were also made on the collections of music at the Los Angeles Public Library, at the Y. M. C. A., Brooklyn, at the Pratt Institute Library, and at the New Haven Public Library. Miss Mildred A. Collar presented a paper on "Book-hunting and bibliophiles."

The Committee on legislation reported that various amendments had been proposed to the Education Bill pending at Albany, and that careful attention had been given to the library provisions of the measure.

The May meeting was held on the 12th in the new Columbia University Library. Mr. Geo. H. Baker described the new building and dwelt upon its special features, including the arrangements of the seminar-rooms. Mr. Bostwick gave an account of the proposed new building for the Bloomingdale Branch of the New York Free Circulating Library, showing the plans for the same. Mr. W. Eames gave an account of the "Early printed books in the New York Public Library." C. Alex. Nelson read a brief paper on "The university library." This being the annual meeting the Teasurer's report was read and audited. The whole board of officers was reëlected for the ensuing year.

The sixty-second meeting of the Club was held Oct. 13th, at the rooms of the Y. M. C. A. on West 57th Street. Dr. J. S. Billings gave an account of "The recent Conference of the L. A. U. K., at Southport, Eng.," at which he was the American representative. The question of open access to shelves proved the only disturbing element in an otherwise peaceful conference. A paper by Miss Mary W. Plummer on "Modern Spanish novelists" was read by Miss Josephine A. Rathbone. Reports from the various libraries on innovations and progress during the past year followed. After some discussion a committee of three was appointed to confer with the New York Library Association and with any library club in the State to devise and propose a plan whereby the library interests of the State may be federated.

On the evening of Nov. 10th, the Club met at the Lenox Library building, Fifth Avenue and 70th Street. The Committee on federation reported progress and asked to be continued. The papers read were arranged to illustrate the special characteristics of the Lenox Library. Mr. Eames presented an "Historical account of the Lenox Library," giving a sketch of the life of James Lenox, the founder. Mr. V. H. Paltsits described "Its book treasures and art rarities." Mr. Axel E. Sylvan explained "Its method of cataloging Incunabula, or 15th century books," and Mr. H. M. Lydenberg followed with an account of "Its historical mss. and prints." "Its map department" was described by Mr. Thomas Letts, and Mr. Charles D. Gillis read a paper on "Its department of American genealogy and local history." The last paper, on "Its musical collections," was read by Miss Mary L. Avery.

Jan. 12, 1899, the Club met in the assembly room of the Boys' High School building, 60 West 13th Street. The special subject for discussion was the "Relations between free libraries and public schools," and a number of principals, teachers, and others interested in school work were present. The subject was first presented by Dr. H. M. Leipziger. Miss Julia Richman, principal of

Grammar School No. 77, spoke on "The reading of school girls," as observed by her, and made some valuable suggestions on the home reading of school children. Miss Mary E. Merington read a practical paper criticising the "Indiscriminate selection of books for public libraries," and urging some method of regulating the issue of books to young people. Miss Emma Cragin gave an account of the "Travelling library department of the N. Y. Free Circulating Library." Miss Moore spoke of the children's use of the University Settlement Library. Mr. Bostwick, Dr. Leipziger, School Commissioner O'Brien, Miss Foote, and Mr. McDowell, of Newark, took part in the discussion. It was voted to hold the annual dinner on Feb. 16th, in connection with the meeting of the State Library Association at Poughkeepsie.

The February meeting was held on the 16th at the Young Women's Christian Association, 7 East 15th Street. On account of the weather, very few out-of-town members of the State Association were present. The Dinner Committee was authorized to spend not more than fifty dollars, and it was voted to hold the next meeting March 17th in conjunction with the Pennsylvania Library Club and the N. J. Library Association, at Atlantic City. The annual topic "Reports of library progress from the various libraries represented in the Club" was opened by Mr. Eastman with a general report on library progress in the State. On behalf of the New York Public Library Mr. Eames reported for the Lenox Library, and Mr. Frank Weitenkampf for the Astor. Miss Pauline Leipziger gave statistics for the Aguilar Library and its new branch. Miss Wallace, of the Cathedral Library, reported a new branch opened in 69th Street. Miss Husted, of the

Y. W. C. A. Library spoke in favor of the open-shelf system as used in that library since its opening. Mr. Bursch reported that funds had been supplied for cataloging the circulating department of the Y. M. C. A. Library. Miss Gibson reported that the St. Agnes Library had been moved to 85th Street and Amsterdam Avenue, and its circulation had increased. Mr. Bostwick stated that the opening of new branches had raised the circulation of the N. Y. Free Circulating Library to about one and a half million volumes a year, and the open-shelf system had literally been forced upon the library by the public. Miss Winser reported that the corner-stone of the new Newark Library building was laid Jan. 26th, and that a number of Polish and Lithuanian books had been added. Mr. Richardson stated that the building at Princeton had been completed and many gifts received. Miss Plummer described changes and improvements at the Pratt Institute, especially in the children's room.

Mr. Peck, of Gloversville, said that he paid less attention to large circulation than to the number of readers, the manner of reading, and the matter read. Other reports of library progress were made by Mrs. F. N. Doubleday and W. F. Stevens, and a written report was read from Miss A. R. Van Hovenberg.

The meeting was followed by a reception and dinner at the Hotel St. Denis. John Jay Chapman was the speaker of the evening and made a strong plea for recognition of individuality and genius in literature.

In accordance with the vote of the Club the March meeting was merged in the tri-state joint meeting with the Pennsylvania and New Jersey State Library Associations held at Atlantic City March 17–18, 1899. The Club was represented in the proceedings of the meeting by Miss Helen E. Haines, who read a short paper entitled, "New lamps for old," drawing attention to some of the older novels; by R. R. Bowker, in an address on "The Library," and its development since the first A. L. A. meeting in 1876; and by Melvil Dewey, who spoke upon the work of the modern librarian in raising educational and artistic standards.

The sixty-seventh and annual meeting was held at the University Settlement Building, Rivington and Delancey Streets, on May 25th. A resolution was passed making membership in the Club include membership in the State Association and *vice versa*. The regular program was opened with a paper by F. W. Halsey, of the *New York Times*, on "Librarians and literary editors—their responsibilities in a deluge." This was followed by short talks on "Methods for making known to the public the existence and work of a library." Miss M. E. Mills, Miss Leipziger, and Miss A. C. Moore were among the speakers. Misses Haines, Kelso, and Hitchler gave some amusing accounts of the social side of the Atlanta meeting of the A. L. A. Officers were elected for the next year.

The Club met October 12th in the parlors of the Y. M. C. A. on 23d Street. President Billings referred to the difficulty of finding subjects for discussion and called on members to suggest new topics. The Executive Committee recommended that the Club undertake the preparation of a library handbook for New York City. C. Alex. Nelson read a paper on "Incunabula in New York City," stating that there were probably nearly 2000 "cradle books" in the various libraries, public and private, the greatest number being found at the Union Theological

Seminary, the New York Public Library, and at Columbia University. A special union card catalog had been begun at Columbia, which included 857 titles. Frank Weitenkampf gave a specially interesting account of "The Ford Collection," recently presented to the New York Public Library. Mr. Bostwick's topic was "Brooklyn libraries," but he confined his remarks to the Brooklyn Public Library and its plans for the future. It was proposed, he said, to cover the Borough of Brooklyn with a network of small circulating libraries, each the centre of a circle having a radius of three quarters of a mile, the circles of adjacent libraries touching at their circumference.

Miss M. W. Plummer described the "Photograph Collection of Pratt Institute Free Library," how the prints were mounted, catalogd, and circulated.

The November meeting was held on the 8th, at the Mercantile Library, with a large attendance. W. T. Peoples read a paper on the "History of the Mercantile Library," showing that the Library had been an important factor in the educational life of the city. Lecture courses were introduced by it in 1827 and continued till 1875. Although still a subscription library several efforts had been made to make it a free institution. F. B. Bigelow read a paper on the "Old newspapers in the Society Library." Mr. Eames and Mr. Paltsits followed with remarks on the old newspapers in the New York Public Library.

A discussion of the topic, "Hours of library service considered from the standpoint of the employee," followed, in which Mr. Wing, Miss Cragin, Miss Winser, Dr. Canfield, Miss Prescott, Miss Husted, Miss Rathbone, Miss Hitchler, W. R. Eastman, and Geo. W. Cole took part.

Dr. Billings summed up the question with the statement that seven hours per day seemed to be proper, with not less than one hour at meal time; he also advocated a yearly vacation of one month. After adjournment a collation was served by the courtesy of Mr. Peoples.

On Jan. 11, 1900, the Club met at the Astor Library Building, at 8.15 P.M. The report of the Executive Committee recommending that no action making for affiliation with the State Library Association be taken at this time was adopted. The topic for discussion was "State library laws." J. N. Wing spoke on the laws of Massachusetts and New York, comparing the provisions of each. R. E. Helbig discussed the laws of New Hampshire and Wisconsin. Miss A. R. Hasse compared the laws of California, Illinois, and Iowa, stating that in 1872 Illinois passed the first full and specific library law. Miss D. S. Pinneo described the library laws of Connecticut, their advantages and defects. W. C. Kimball referred to the movement for a State library commission in New Jersey developed by the State Library Association, and Miss L. E. Stearns spoke of the work of the Wisconsin Commission.

The second topic, "Cheaper postage for library books," was postponed until the next meeting.

A meeting of the Club was held Feb. 8th, at Columbia University, where Dr. Canfield made an address of welcome. The first two papers on the program, "The best methods of work with adults in free libraries," by Mrs. Agnes Hills, and "The difficulties of systematic training of school children in the use of the library and of reference books," by Miss Agnes Wallace, were omitted owing to the absence of the authors. A paper by J. C. Sickley, of Poughkeepsie, was read by J. N. Wing, describing the writer's efforts to interest school children in the use of reference books and books bearing upon their studies.

An animated discussion on the relation of the school to the library followed. Mr. Wing stated that travelling libraries were supplied to the schools, the books being used as supplementary readers. Mr. Bostwick remarked that nine tenths of the teachers looked askance at librarians. The question was finally left open for future action.

Miss Harriet Husted read an interesting paper on "Open shelves in the Y. W. C. A. of New York." Miss Plummer sent some statistics regarding the open-shelf experiment at Pratt Institute Free Library. The question of "Reduced postage for library books" was discussed by A. E. Bostwick and R. R. Bowker, and a paper against the proposed reduction, by C. Alex. Nelson, was read by J. T. Gerould.

The Club united with the State Library Association at its mid-year meeting on March 8th. The sessions were held at the hall of the Y. W. C. A. on East 15th Street. Dr. John S. Billings made a brief address of welcome, regretting that his health would prevent his fulfilling his duties as President of the Club. Dr. Canfield introduced C. H. Gould, of the McGill University, Montreal, who extended an earnest invitation to all to attend the meeting of the A. L. A. in that city. George Watson Cole then opened the regular program with a paper on "Library development in New York State, 1800–1900." H. L. Elmendorf, of Buffalo, read a paper on "The relation of the public library to the public school," followed by W. R. Eastman and Edwin W. Gaillard on the same topic. "The books of 1899" were introduced by Miss M. M. Monachesi, who reviewed the classes of Biography,

History, and Poetry. Miss Hewins discussed her favorite subject, the "Children's books," and "Fiction" was considered by Miss Eleanor Woodruff, of Pratt Institute.

F. B. Bigelow, vice-president of the Club, presided at the afternoon session. Robert Rutter presented a paper on "The development of bookbinding in New York City," illustrated by binding implements and a book in the process of binding. George Haven Putnam gave an address on "The evolution of a book," showing complete knowledge of the subject. Arthur W. Tyler gave a brief talk, "Gleanings from twenty-five years of library experience." The closing topic, "The St. Louis plan for meeting the demand for popular fiction," was opened by C. Alex. Nelson, who read the account of the duplicate collection of popular fiction issued on the payment of a small fee as given by F. M. Crunden in *The Library*. Miss Plummer sent a statement of the system as adopted at Pratt Institute, and W. A. Borden described its working at the Young Men's Institute of New Haven, Ct.

In the evening the Club celebrated its fifteenth anniversary with a dinner at the rooms of the Aldine Association, Fifth Avenue and 18th Street. In the absence of Dr. Billings, Dr. J. H. Canfield presided as toast-master. Among the speakers were R. G. Thwaites, president of the A. L. A., Herbert Putnam, W. C. Lane, F. W. Halsey, Dr. Morris Jastrow, Dr. E. C. Richardson, Miss M. E. Hazeltine, Miss Hewins, and Madame Magnússon, (wife of Eiríkr Magnússon, deputy librarian of Cambridge University, Eng.), "whose reluctant little speech was one of the successes of the evening." "Taken as a whole, the joint meeting was probably the most notable in the history of the bodies represented."

The fifteenth annual and seventy-third meeting of the Club was held at the Aguilar Free Library, May 10, 1900, at 3 P.M., Dr. J. S. Billings presiding. After the annual election of officers the regular program was opened with a paper on "Early American imprints," by W. J. James.* Miss Elizabeth L. Foote presented a paper on "Apprentices in libraries," followed by Miss Theresa Hitchler on the same subject. The program closed with a paper entitled "Volumes and circulation, a study in percentages," by Arthur E. Bostwick.

The October meeting was held on the 11th at the Y. M. C. A. building on 23d Street. The subject for discussion was "The relation of the libraries to the Educational Department of the City," and a large number of persons interested in educational matters was present. J. N. Wing gave a full account of the work done for the schools by the New York Free Circulating Library, stating that now nearly a hundred travelling libraries were sent to the schools and many club classes. Mr. Gaillard, of the Webster Library, explained the very practical methods he had adopted to reach teachers and pupils of the schools in its vicinity. Rev. Father McMahon, of the Cathedral Library, emphasized the guiding power and influence of the teacher and urged that the library be not exaggerated but that more attention be given to the schools. Dr. Leipziger urged the need of training teachers to use the libraries and of extending the work of coöperation. Mr. Burlingham, of the School Board, pleaded that the child be allowed to browse among the books, familiarity with them often developing a love for good reading. He

* This paper was printed in full in the *Publishers' Weekly* for May 19, 1900.

explained the system of school libraries in use by the School Board, the tendency being to class libraries. The great need was the personal contact of the librarian and the teacher. Mr. Eastman closed the subject with a hope that the liberty of the child would always be recognized.

A vote was passed instructing the Executive Committee to invite to a conference representatives of the New York High School Teachers' Association, and of any other teachers' association or organization existing in the city in connection with the public schools.

The seventy-fifth meeting of the Club, and the last meeting of the century, was held November 8th, at the Y. M. C. A. building on 23d Street. George W. Cole, chairman of the Committee on printing the new Handbook of the Club, gave an outline of the plan adopted by the Committee in regard to the data to be given in the Handbook. Section three of the Constitution was amended so as to grant membership in the Club to all institutions having libraries or interested in library work. Miss Mary W. Plummer gave a talk on "Some impressions of the International Congress of Librarians at Paris." Dr. James H. Canfield reported from the Special Committee on coöperation between free libraries and public schools certain recommendations, of which the following were adopted: That of the bulletins issued by the various libraries, a reasonable number should be sent to the principal of each school, for the use of the teachers in that school; that the Club devote one of its meetings each year, preferably the first, to a discussion of this question of the coöperation of the libraries and the schools; that the Club request the various teachers' associations of this city, which discuss educational questions, to devote one meeting a year to a discussion of the possible coöperation of the schools and libraries, and to invite the librarians of the city to be present at these meetings.

The present "Historical Sketch" finds a fitting close with the end of the century, during the last fifteen years of which the Club has pursued its career of uninterrupted success. The published records of its Proceedings have been good seed, which have fallen into good ground and have produced an abundant harvest. Its work has supplemented and emphasized that of its only predecessor, the great parent of all library clubs, the American Library Association. The latter, by its general meetings, held almost annually since 1876, has blazed its way across the continent from The Thousand Islands to the Golden Gate, from Sault Ste. Marie to the delta of the Mississippi, and from Mt. Washington to Pike's Peak and Lookout Mountain, and in its track have sprung up no less than thirty State and general library associations, and twenty-one State library commissions, all organized and established since 1890. Twelve sister library clubs have likewise followed in the footsteps of their illustrious predecessor, whose pioneer work seems to have been begun but yesterday.

The American library spirit crossed the Atlantic in 1877, and from the United Kingdom spread to the Continent, to India and to Australasia; westward too it has taken its way and "put a girdle round about the earth," for Japan has a "Western Library Association."

With such a past, notable as it has been, the New York Library Club can not rest content; it must take cognizance of the great opportunities which the immediate future gives promise of, and prepare to meet the great responsibilities which devolve upon it. It must remain in the vanguard of all library progress; it must stand for only the best in all departments of library work; it must live up to its unwritten motto, "the highest our only standard."

MEMBERS

OF THE

NEW YORK LIBRARY CLUB

Date following name indicates year of joining. * Charter Members.

ADAMS, BENJAMIN (1900) Brooklyn Public Library, Prospect Branch, 128 State Street, Brooklyn.

AGNEW, MISS L. N. (1902) 3 East 9th Street, New York City.

ANTHONY, JULIA B. (1892) Packer Collegiate Institute, Brooklyn.

APPLETON, WILLIAM W. (1885) 72 Fifth Ave., New York City.

ARDEN, HARRIETTE (1898) Y. W. C. A., 7 East 15th Street, New York City.

AVERY, MARY L. (1898) N. Y. P. L., 40 Lafayette Place, New York City.

BABCOCK, L. ELLA (1896) Library of Congress, Washington, D. C.

BAKER, GEORGE HALL (1886) 294 Manhattan Ave., New York City.

BALDWIN, ELIZABETH G. (1889) Teachers College, West 120th Street, New York City.

BALDWIN, EMMA V. (1899). B. P. L., 26 Brevoort Place, Brooklyn.

BANKS, MRS. MARTHA HOWARD GORDON (1889) Dyer Library, Saco, Maine.

BARDWELL, WILLIS ARTHUR (1885) B. P. L., 26 Brevoort Place, Brooklyn.

BATE, FLORENCE E. (1901) McClure, Phillips & Co., 141-155 East 25th Street, New York City.

BATE, MARIAN (1900) 40 Wall Street, New York City.

BAYS, EMMA A. (1901) St. George's Parish Library, 207 East 16th Street, New York City.

BEDELL, MRS. DELL BURBECK (1890) Free Public Library, Newark, N. J.

BERRY, SILAS HURD (1885) Library of Y. M. C. A., 318 West 57th Street, New York City.

BIGELOW, FRANK BARNA (1894) Society Library, 109 University Place, New York City.

BILLINGS, JOHN SHAW, M.D., LL.D. (1896) New York Public Library, Astor Building, 40 Lafayette Place, New York City.

BISHOP, WILLIAM WARNER (1901) Polytechnic Institute, Brooklyn.

BOGGAN, EVA (1901) Webster Free Library, 76th Street and East River, New York City.

BOGGAN, MARY (1901) 251 West 13th Street, N. Y. City.

BOSTWICK, ARTHUR ELMORE, Ph.D. (1895) N. Y. P. L., Circulation Dep't, 226 West 42d Street, New York City.

BOWKER, RICHARD ROGERS (1885) 274 Lafayette Avenue, Brooklyn.

BRAINERD, FANNY P. (1896) B. P. L., Schermerhorn Street Branch, 67 Schermerhorn Street, Brooklyn.

BREWER, MISS F. B. (1902) Woodycrest Avenue, 162d Street, New York City.

BROWN, ADELINE EXPERIENCE (1894) N. Y. P. L., Travelling Library Dep't, 206 West 100th Street, New York City.

BROWN, ALICE H. (1894) N. Y. P. L., Harlem Branch, 218 East 125th Street, New York City.

BROWN, HARRIET D. (1901) 120 East 34th Street, and Columbia University Library.

BUCHANAN, JAMES D. (1886) 328 West 24th Street, New York City.

BUCKNAM, EDITH (1901) N. Y. P. L., Astor Building, 40 Lafayette Place, New York City.

BURDICK, ESTHER ELIZABETH (1891) Public Library, Jersey City, N. J.

BURLINGHAM, CHARLES C. (1900) 59th Street and Park Avenue, New York City.

BURSCH, FREDERICK C. (1898) New York City.

BURSCH, MRS. FREDERICK C., *née* DENNIS (1898) 60 West 101st Street, New York City.

CANFIELD, JAMES HULME, LL.D. (1899) Columbia University Library, New York City.

CANFIELD, MARIAN (1901) Arthur Winter Memorial Library, New Brighton, S. I.

CARY, MRS. CORNELIA H. (1896) 33 Pierrepont Street, Brooklyn.

CAULFIELD, MISS B. M. H. (1902) Woodycrest Avenue, High Bridge, New York City.

CLARKE, HOWARD, (1899) 280 Broadway, New York City.

CLARKE, MARY E. (1900) B. P. L., Flatbush Branch, 7 Caton Avenue, Brooklyn.

CLARKE, RALPH G. (1891) 21 East Houston St., N. Y. City.

COLE, GEORGE WATSON (1888) Graham Court, 1925 Seventh Avenue, New York City.

COMBA, THEOPHILE ERNEST (1896) 67 Fifth Avenue, New York City.

COOMBES, GEORGE J., (1899) N. Y. P. L., Astor Building, 40 Lafayette Place, New York City.

CORWIN, DR. BELLE (1898) New York University Library, Riverside Terrace, New York City.

CRAGIN, EMMA F. (1890) N. Y. P. L., Circulation Dep't, 226 West 42d Street, New York City.

CRAIGIE, MRS. MARY E. (1896) 143 Linden Avenue, Flatbush, N. Y.

CRANSTON, MRS. MARY (1901) League for Social Service, Charities Building, 22d Street and 4th Avenue, New York City.

CROSS, MRS. RICHARD JAMES (1886) 6 Washington Square, New York City.

CURTIS, GEORGE DE CLYVER (1900) N. Y. P. L., Lenox Building, 890 Fifth Avenue, New York City.

DAVIDSON, HERBERT E. (1891) 377 Broadway, New York City.

DAVIE, ELEANOR ELIZABETH (1897) Educational Dep't, Harper & Bros., Franklin Square, New York City.

DAVIS, MARY LOUISE (1896) Pratt Institute Free Library, Ryerson Street, Brooklyn.

DE MORGAN, JOHN (1901) New Brighton, S. I.

DONEGHY, GRACE (1902) B. P. L., Tompkins Park Branch, Brooklyn

DOUBLEDAY, MRS. FRANK N. (1902) 111 East 16th Street, New York City.

DUNCAN, WILLIAM HENRY, JR. (1899) Library of University Club, 54th Street and Fifth Ave., N. Y. City.

EAMES, WILBERFORCE, A. M. (1895) N. Y. P. L., Lenox Building, 890 Fifth Avenue, New York City.

EASTMAN, REV. WILLIAM REED (1895) New York State Library, Albany. N. Y.

EGER, BERTHA (1895) N. Y. P. L., Astor Building, 40 Lafayette Place, New York City.

ERB, FREDERIC WILLIAM (1901) 520 West 123d Street, and Columbia University Library.

FANNAN, MARY ELEANOR (1896) Free Public Library, Newark, N. J.

FARR, MABEL A. (1891) Adelphi College, Lafayette Avenue, Brooklyn.

FISH, FANNY DEAN (1895) Y. W. C. A., Schermerhorn Street and Flatbush Avenue, Brooklyn.

FOOTE, ELIZABETH LOUISA (1898) N. Y. P. L., Astor Building, 40 Lafayette Place, New York City.

FOSTER, RAE (1901) 498 East 143d Street, and Columbia University Library.

FREIDUS, ABRAHAM SOLOMON (1894) N. Y. P. L., Astor Building, 40 Lafayette Place, New York City.

GAILLARD, EDWIN WHITE (1898) Webster Free Library, 76th Street and East River, New York City.

GARDNER, JULIA H. (1901) N. Y. P. L., Washington Heights Branch, 156th Street and St. Nicholas Ave., New York City.

GAY, HELEN KILDUFF (1896) Mount Vernon Public Library, Mount Vernon, N. Y.

GIBSON, ANNA L. (1896) N. Y. P. L., St. Agnes Branch, 2279 Broadway, New York City.

GIBSON, MARGARET J. (1900) N. Y. P. L., Harlem Branch, 218 East 125th Street, New York City.

GOEKS, MISS HEDWIG M. (1898) N. Y. P. L., Ottendorfer Branch, 135 Second Avenue, New York City.

GOLDTHWAITE, LUCILE (1900) N. Y. P. L., Bruce Branch, 226 West 42d Street, New York City.

GREGOOR, SERVAAS (1901) N. Y. P. L., Astor Building, 40 Lafayette Place, New York City.

GRIMM, MINERVA E. (1899) N. Y. P. L., Yorkville Branch, 1523 Second Avenue, New York City.

GROWOLL, ADOLPH (1885) 298 Broadway, New York City.

HACKETT, IRENE A. (1897) Y. W. C. A., 502 Fulton Street, Brooklyn.

HAINES, HELEN ELIZABETH (1894) The Library Journal, 298 Broadway, New York City.

HAINES, MARTHA BELL (1890) Free Public Library, Newark, N. J.

HALL, MISS M. A. (1899) Pratt Institute Free Library, Ryerson Street, Brooklyn.

HARTICH, MRS. ALICE (1900) B. P. L., Bushwick Branch, 198 Montrose Avenue, Brooklyn.

HASSE, ADELAIDE ROSALIE (1898) N. Y. P. L., Astor Building, 40 Lafayette Place, New York City.

HATFIELD, THOMAS FRANCIS (1891) Free Public Library, Hoboken, N. J.

HAWLEY, FRANCES B. (1899) B. P. L., 26 Brevoort Place, Brooklyn.

HELBIG, RICHARD ERNEST (1899) N. Y. P. L., Lenox Building, 890 Fifth Avenue, New York City.

HERSHFIELD, MISS L. N. (1901) Aguilar Free Library, 9 West 121st Street, New York City.

HERZOG, ALFRED C. (1891) Free Public Library, Bayonne, N. J.

HIFTON, HARRIETTE (1900) Mercantile Library, 15 Astor Place, New York City.

HILL, FRANK PIERCE (1889) Brooklyn Public Library, 26 Brevoort Place, Brooklyn.

HILLEBRAND, HELEN (1900) 226 West 42d Street, New York City.

HILLS, MRS. AGNES (1893) Public Library, Bridgeport, Conn.

HITCHLER, THERESA (1890) B. P. L., 26 Brevoort Place, Brooklyn.

HOWE, LAURA (1901) Salem Centre, Westchester Co., N. Y.

HOWELL, RODNEY T. (1895) West Shore Railroad Y. M. C. A., Weehawken, N. J.

HULL, FANNY (1886) B. P. L., Schermerhorn Street Branch, 67 Schermerhorn Street, Brooklyn.

HULL, MARY A. (1892) Bath Beach, Brooklyn.

HUME, JESSIE F. (1897) Queens Borough Public Library, Long Island City, N. Y.

HUSTED, HARRIET (1898) Y. W. C. A., 7 East 15th Street, New York City.

HUSTIS, MRS. HENRY HAIGHT (1890) 32A Baldwin Street, Newark, N. J.

JACKSON, MRS. ESTELLE (1902) B. P. L., Bedford Park Branch, 185 Brooklyn Avenue, Brooklyn.

JACOBSEN, KATRINA H. (1900) B. P. L., City Park Branch, 186 Bridge Street, Brooklyn.

JAMES, WILLIAM JOHN, A.M. (1894) Wesleyan University, Middletown, Conn.

JEFFRIES, REV. MORTIMER TOWNSEND (1895) American Society of Civil Engineers, 127 East 23d Street, New York City.

JOHNSON, FREDERICK B. (1900) Library Bureau, 377 Broadway, New York City.

JOOS, GUSTAV (1900) N. Y. P. L., Astor Building, 40 Lafayette Place, New York City.

JUDD, LEWIS STRONG, Jr. (1892) N. Y. P. L., Astor Building, 40 Lafayette Place, New York City.

KELSO, TESSA L. (1896) Baker-Taylor Co., 33 East 17th Street, New York City.

KEMP, MISS E. E. (1902) 33 Wall Street (Blair & Co.) New York City,

KENNEY, JOSEPHINE (1890) Free Public Library, Newark, N. J.

KENT, HENRY W. (1901) Grolier Club, 29 East 32d Street, New York City.

KERNOCHAN, JOSEPH FREDERIC (1886) 11 East 26th Street, New York City.

KIMBALL, WILLIAM C. (1897) Trustee, Public Library, Passaic, N. J., 96 Prince Street, New York City.

LEIPZIGER, HENRY MARCUS, PH.D. (1892) 324 East 50th Street, New York City.

LEIPZIGER, PAULINE (1893) Aguilar Free Library, 113 East 59th Street, New York City.

LEMCKE, ERNEST (1896) 812 Broadway, New York City.

LETTS, THOMAS (1899) N. Y. P. L., Lenox Building, 890 Fifth Avenue, New York City.

LEVY, MRS. SARAH LANG (1898) 948 Park Avenue, New York City.

LITHGOW, GEORGE W. (1886) 41 King Street, N. Y. City.

LYDENBERG, HARRY MILLER (1897) N. Y. P. L., Astor Building, 40 Lafayette Place, New York City.

McDOWELL, WILLIAM O. (1891) Room 121, 115 Broadway, New York City.

McMAHON, REV. JOSEPH H. (1900) Madison Avenue and 51st Street, New York City.

MACMILLAN, MARY (1900) B. P. L., South Brooklyn Branch, 1147 Fourth Avenue, Brooklyn.

MACMULLEN, GRACE L. (1900) 479 West 152d Street, New York City, and Columbia University Library.

MAITLAND, ALEXANDER (1900) 14 East 55th Street, New York City.

MANN, ELIZABETH ELLEN (1902) Columbia University Library, New York City.

MARSH, LILIAN ADELAIDE (1891) Free Public Library, Newark, N. J.

MEADE, CHARLOTTE (1900) N. Y. P. L., Geo. Bruce Branch, 226 West 42d Street, New York City.

MEIGS, ALICE (1901) B. P. L., 26 Brevoort Place, Brooklyn.

MILLER, MARY EMILY (1894) Library Equitable Life Insurance Co., 120 Broadway, New York City.

MILLS, ELEANOR (1898) N. Y. P. L., Yorkville Branch, 1523 Second Avenue, New York City.

MONTGOMERY, THOMAS L. (1891) Wagner Free Institute of Science, Philadelphia, Pa.

MORAND, PAULINE JULIA MARTHA (1898) N. Y. P. L., Astor Building, 40 Lafayette Place, New York City.

MULLINS, JOHN DAVIES (1887) honorary member, Free Library, Birmingham, England.

MURRAY, EDGAR SMITH, (1900) N. Y. P. L., Astor Building, 40 Lafayette Place, New York City.

NATHAN, MADELINE (1896) Aguilar Free Library, 197 East Broadway, New York City.

* NELSON, CHARLES ALEXANDER, A. M. (1885) Columbia University Library, New York City.

NEUMANN, CHARLES C. (1890) 7 East 16th St., N. Y. City.

ODDIE, SARAH SLATER (1896) East Orange Public Library, East Orange, N. J.

ODELL, HELEN PARSONS (1894) B. P. L., Williamsburg Branch, 474 Bedford Avenue, Brooklyn.

O'MEARA, ELLEN H. (1896) Aguilar Free Library, 113 East 59th Street, New York City.

PALTSITS, VICTOR HUGO (1896) N. Y. P. L., Lenox Building, 890 Fifth Avenue, New York City.

PARKER, S. R. (1902) Cooper Union, Astor Place, New York City.

*PEOPLES, WILLIAM THADDEUS (1885) Mercantile Library, 15 Astor Place, New York City.

PERRY, GEORGE MURDOCK (1893) 16 West 128th Street, New York City, and General Theological Seminary, Ninth Avenue and 20th Street.

PETRIE, MISS F. R. (1898) Y. M. C. A., 317 West 56th Street, New York City.

PHILLIPS, CHARLES FRANÇOIS (1896) 52 Broadway, New York City.

PHILLIPS, GRACE L. (1899) University Settlement Library, Rivington Street, New York City.

PINNEO, DOTHA S. (1898) City of Norwalk Public Library, Norwalk, Conn.

PLUMMER, MARY WRIGHT (1890) Pratt Institute Free Library, Ryerson Street, Brooklyn.

POWELL, HELEN L. (1899) Nyack Free Library, Nyack, N. Y.

PRESCOTT, HARRIET BEARDSLEE (1890) Columbia University Library, New York City.

PROPER, IDA S. (1901) Mechanics' Institute Free Library, West 44th Street, New York City.

PROSSER, HARRIET R. (1900) Englewood, N. J.

RATHBONE, JOSEPHINE ADAMS (1893) Pratt Institute Free Library, Ryerson Street, Brooklyn.

RICHARDSON, REV. ERNEST CUSHING (1890) Princeton University Library, Princeton, N. J.

ROBERTS, JAMES L., (1899) Baker-Taylor Co., 5 East 16th Street, New York City.

ROCKWOOD, MRS. WILLIAM HEWITT (1897) 513 West End Avenue, New York City.

ROE, MARY ELIZABETH (1896) 310 Lafayette Avenue, Brooklyn.

ROSENTHAL, HERMANN (1899) N. Y. P. L., Astor Building, 40 Lafayette Place, New York City.

ROURKE, MISS M. P. (1902) Cathedral Library, 123 East 50th Street, New York City.

RUTTER, ROBERT (1886) 141 East 25th Street, New York City.

*RYLANCE, MRS. JOSEPH H., *née* COE (1885) 11 Livingston Place, New York City.

SAUER, ELLA M. (1894) N. Y. P. L., Circulation Dep't, 226 West 42d Street, New York City.

SAXER, MARIE C. (1894) N. Y. P. L., Bond Street Branch, 49 Bond Street, New York City.

SCHOFIELD, LURA B. (1900) B. P. L., Williamsburg Branch, 474 Bedford Avenue, Brooklyn.

SCHOTTENFELS, SARA X. (1894) Maimonides Free Library, 723 Lexington Avenue, New York City.

SEE, CORNELIA A. (1890) Free Public Library, New Brunswick, N. J.

SHELDON, FANNY A. (1901) B. P. L., 369 Madison Street, Brooklyn.

SICKLEY, JOHN C. (1895) Public Library, Poughkeepsie, N. Y.

SIEDLER, MISS M. E. (1902) N. Y. P. L., Astor Building, 40 Lafayette Place, New York City.

SMILEY, ANNETTE F., (1899) 317 West 56th Street, New York City.

SMITH, BESSIE S. (1898) late Harlem Library, 123d Street and Lenox Avenue, New York City.

SMITH, TILLIE J. (1899) Free Public Library, Newark, N. J.

SPEIRS, CHARLES EDWARD (1891) 23 Murray Street, New York City.

STEIGER, ERNST (1886) 25 Park Place, New York City.

STEINBERGER, MATILDA HILDEGARDE (1894) N. Y. P. L., Chatham Square Branch, 22 East Broadway, New York City.

STETSON, WILLIS KIMBALL (1891) Free Public Library, New Haven, Conn.

STEVENS, FREDERIC WILLIAM (1901) 33 West 35th Street, New York City.

SULZBERGER, CYRUS L. (1900) 58 West 87th Street, New York City.

SULZBERGER, MRS. CYRUS L. (1900) 58 West 87th Street, New York City.

SUNDERLAND, J. L. B. (1894) Library of Railroad Men's Branch, Y. M. C. A., Hoboken, N. J.

TALMAGE, KATE V. N. (1898) 367 Lenox Road, Brooklyn.

TEMLETT, LOUISE (1901) 29 Pennsylvania Avenue, Brooklyn.

THAYER, ANNIE M. (1901) B. P. L., 209 Carroll Street, Brooklyn.

THOMAS, REV. JOSEPH CONABLE (1894) Methodist Library, 150 Fifth Avenue, New York City.

THOMPSON, LIDA V. (1901) B. P. L., Astral Branch, Java and Franklin Streets, and 13 Arlington Place, Brooklyn.

THORNE, CAROLYN G. (1900) Harlem Library, 32 West 123d Street, New York City.

TOBEY, GRACE (1901) B. P. L., 26 Brevoort Place, Brooklyn.

TODD, CHARLOTTE A. (1898) B. P. L., Schermerhorn Street Branch, 67 Schermerhorn Street, Brooklyn.

TOEDTEBERG, EMMA (1886) Long Island Historical Society, Pierrepont, corner Clinton Street, Brooklyn.

TOWNSEND, LUCILE R. (1901) N. Y. P. L., Astor Building, 40 Lafayette Place, New York City.

TUTTLE, ELIZABETH (1886) Long Island Historical Society, Pierrepont, corner Clinton Street, Brooklyn.

ULMANN, ALICE M. (1900) Y. W. C. A., 7 East 15th Street, New York City.

VAN HOEVENBERG, ALMA ROGERS (1893) N. Y. P. L., Washington Heights Branch, St. Nicholas Avenue and 156th Street, New York City.

VAN HOEVENBERG, ELIZABETH (1893) The Ferguson Library, Stamford, Conn.

VAN NAME, ADDISON (1898) Yale University Library, New Haven, Conn.

WAIT, MARIE FOX (1896) New Jersey Historical Society, Newark, N. J.

WALLACE, AGNES (1899) Cathedral Library, 123 East 50th Street, New York City.

WALLER, PERCY (1898) N. Y. P. L., Lenox Building, 890 Fifth Avenue, New York City.

WALLIS, MARY V. (1895) N. Y. P. L., Astor Building, 40 Lafayette Place, New York City.

WASHBURNE, MRS. OLIVE B. (1896) Methodist Library, 150 Fifth Avenue, New York City.

WATERMAN, LUCY D. (1899) Library New York Law School, 35 Nassau Street, New York City.

WATTERSON, ROBERTA F. (1897) Free Public Library, South Orange, N. J.

WEITENKAMPF, FRANK (1895) N. Y. P. L., Astor Building, 40 Lafayette Place, New York City.

WELSH, R. G. (1900) Chas. Scribner's Sons, 153-157 Fifth Avenue, New York City.

WESSON, ELIZABETH HOWLAND (1899) Orange Free Library, Orange, N. J.

*WHITE, WILLIAM AUGUSTUS (1885) 158 Columbia Heights, Brooklyn.

WHITTLE, JOHN J. (1898) N. Y. P. L., Lenox Building, 980 Fifth Avenue, New York City.

WILDE, ALICE (1901) N. Y. P. L., Washington Heights Branch, St. Nicholas Avenue, 156th Street, New York City.

WILDMAN, BERTHA S. (1900) Public Library, Madison, N. J.

WILLIAMS, OLIVE A. (1900) Columbia University Library, University Heights, New York City.

WILLSON, S. C. (1901) N. Y. P. L., St. Agnes Branch, 2279 Broadway, New York City.

WINCHESTER, GEORGE F. (1889) Free Public Library, Paterson, N. J.

WINSER, BEATRICE (1890) Free Public Library, Newark, N. J.

WIRE, GEORGE, M.D. (1889) Worcester Co. Law Library, Worcester, Mass.

WITHAM, ELIZA (1901) B. P. L., 85 Java Street, Brooklyn.

WOODRUFF, ELEANOR BERRY (1895) Pratt Institute Free Library, Ryerson Street, Brooklyn.

WOODWARD, ANTHONY, Ph.D. (1901) American Museum Natural History, 77th Street and Eighth Avenue, New York City.

YERKES, SUSAN H. (1890) Arthur Winter Memorial Library, Tompkinsville, Staten Island, N. Y.

www.ingramcontent.com/pod-product-compliance
Lightning Source LLC
LaVergne TN
LVHW011225110826
845150LV00006B/1554

* 9 7 8 1 4 2 5 5 1 6 5 7 4 *